The 1922 General Election Reconsidered

History & Policy Shorts

History & Policy Shorts is a series of concise, open access books designed to foster dialogue between professional historians and policymakers, providing concrete examples of how history and historical reasoning can assist in finding answers to major contemporary problems.

Published in association with History & Policy (H&P) at the Institute of Historical Research, the series builds on H&P's decades of excellence in open access publishing, contributing timely and succinct historical insights into the policy issues of the present. In an era of government characterised by limited institutional memory and insufficient opportunities to consider problems in their historical contexts, there is an urgent need for more communication between academics and policymakers. The series' books are therefore essential reading both for historians looking to understand the nature of policymaking and engaging policymakers with their research, and for policymakers who want to explore how historical research can enrich their work.

The series features accessible, short-form publications (20,000–50,000 words) across three main strands:

1. Books on a wide variety of historical topics, tailored to demonstrate their relevance to current political and policy concerns.
2. Books exploring the workings, past and present, of specific UK government departments.
3. Books examining how and to what extent history can usefully feed into the policymaking process.

Series editors

Philip Murphy, Professor of British and Commonwealth History and Director of History and Policy, Institute of Historical Research, University of London, UK; Simon Szreter, Professor of History and Public Policy and Fellow of St John's College, University of Cambridge, UK; Laura King, Professor of Collaborative History, University of Leeds, UK.

INSTITUTE OF HISTORICAL RESEARCH | SCHOOL OF ADVANCED STUDY UNIVERSITY OF LONDON | HISTORY & POLICY

The 1922 General Election Reconsidered

High Politics and the Birth of the Modern British Election

G.H. Bennett

UNIVERSITY OF LONDON PRESS

Available to purchase in print or download
for free at https://uolpress.co.uk

First published 2025 by
University of London Press
Senate House, Malet St, London WC1E 7HU

A CIP catalogue record for this book is available from The British Library.

ISBN 9781914477706 (hardback)
ISBN 9781914477713 (paperback)
ISBN 9781914477744 (.epub)
ISBN 9781914477737 (.pdf)
ISBN 9781914477720 (.html)

DOI https://doi.org/10.63674/djye2279

Cover image: Photo by Lorenzo Spoleti on Unsplash.

Cover design for University of London Press by Nicky Borowiec.
Series design by Nicky Borowiec.
Book design by Nigel French.
Text set by Westchester Publishing Services, UK in Source Sans Pro,
designed by Paul D. Hunt.

To the colleagues I have known over my career.
We have fought the good fight and we have kept the faith.

Farewell and I'll see you down the road.

Contents

List of tables

Acknowledgements

In the production of this volume, I am indebted to the Lloyd George Archive and particularly to Tony O'Connor for prompting me to take a closer look at the events of the 1922 General Election. I would also like to acknowledge the help and assistance of the staff at the Parliamentary Archives, Churchill College Cambridge, Cambridge University Library, Plymouth University Library, Exeter University Library, the Record Offices at the Isle of Wight Record Office, Bristol Record Office, Kresen Kernow, Devon Record Office, Kent Archive Service, Shropshire Archives, Lancashire Record Office, Liverpool Record Office, Sussex Record Office, London Metropolitan Archives, Dorset History Centre, the Scottish Record Office, the Gloucester Archives, and the Somerset Heritage Centre in supplying materials to contextualise and question the received wisdom from the secondary sources of the 1922 General Election. In reproducing material, despite every effort, it has not been possible to trace and contact every copyright holder, but if they should contact me, I shall see that appropriate acknowledgement is made in any future edition or reprint.

Introduction

General elections, fossilising long-term trends and short-term factors, are the events by which we can chart the evolution of the British political system. The shifting loyalties of voters, the changing fortunes of the parties, the success or failure of leaders, shifts in policy platforms and the impact of the media, together with longer-term social and economic changes across the country, are equally revealed and crystallised into immutable evidence of the political past to be excavated and analysed by psephologists and political historians. Elections matter both in their political outcomes, but also in their contribution to our understanding of the evolution of British politics. The fact that they are dotted throughout decades of British history since the Parliament Act of 1911 decreed that a Parliament could not last longer than five years provides handily spaced datum points for the political historian. Twenty-five elections were held in Britain across a twentieth century in which women and working-class men were finally enfranchised, the voting age was lowered to eighteen, the Liberal Party declined and the Labour Party rose to become the second party of government. Yet these datum points are not equally as regular, or as valuable and reliable, as might be ideal for the political historian.

The two world wars resulted in the postponement of the elections which should have been held no later than 1916 and then also in 1940. This magnifies the importance as datum points of the elections that were eventually held in 1918 and 1945. Yet those elections themselves were both impacted by war, in the case of 1918 severely so, resulting in a turnout of 57.2 per cent: a record low in British general elections in the period 1918–2024. This is particularly unfortunate for the historian interested in trying to understand how the parties were responding to the 1918 Representation of the People

Act with its dramatic widening of the franchise, or the impacts of the First World War on the socio-economic base of British politics, or the process by which the Liberal Party was giving way to the Labour Party. The fact that three other general elections were held in 1922, 1923 and 1924 indicates the extent to which British politics was in flux in the aftermath of the First World War. By the end of that period the pattern for modern British politics of Conservatives and Labour rivalling each other, and with the Liberals a distant third, had become established. It is then a pivotal period in British political history, and if 1918 is less than ideal as a datum point, then that perhaps places an additional emphasis on the 1922 General Election, with its turnout a respectable seventy-three per cent. This would be the first in a critical series of elections in the early 1920s which saw profound changes in the outcomes of the vote from one to another, evidencing fundamental shifts in British politics.

It is the contention of this book that the 1922 General Election was, indeed, the first 'modern' British general election in which the vast majority of the adult population of the United Kingdom was enfranchised, and turned out to vote on a single day, for political parties easily recognisable one hundred years later, in constituency-based, first-past-the-post contests, in an event that felt truly national as a result of a national British media being able to report on the election as it was taking place, and as the results were coming in. In effect, the election took a form and shape still easily recognisable a century later. It is also the contention of this book that the election has not been fully understood by historians, and that has a wider significance because the 1922 election is one of those datum points used to evidence vital long-term trends that were transforming British politics in the early twentieth century. If the datum point is improperly understood then its usefulness as a reference point in charting this process of rapid change is problematic, especially when it is so closely followed by two other datum points (the general elections of 1923 and 1924), and where psephological approaches create an apparent certainty of numbers in the midst of the human realities and chaos and confusion of an election outcome. If the evidence from the 1922 General Election is problematic, in some ways, then, the processes and rates of political change from one election to the next after the First World War may be obscured to the point of creating a false picture. What may appear to be dramatic change in a matter of months may be a more gradual change hidden beneath the illusion of a problematic datum point in 1922.

Why might that election be problematic in some ways, and why might political scientists and historians have had difficulties in interpreting it? Why are there potential issues understanding the data for that election over any other? The problem lies in the fact that to a fundamental extent there was a comprehensive attempt to 'manage' the outcome of the election by the leaderships of two of the political parties (that went well beyond the limited evidence of party pacts operating in Scotland and Lancashire which have been previously recognised), in order to shut out Labour hopes of a dramatic national breakthrough at the polls. In that managed outcome the parties were only partially successful and the outcome was a victory for the Conservatives that was almost completely unexpected, with significant long-term consequences for the Liberal and Labour Parties. Those consequences would further become apparent in the 1923 and 1924 General Elections. In effect, in 1922, while the Labour Party would be seen to be breaking through with the electorate in places like Glasgow, Manchester and Sheffield, the party's wider traction with the electorate was obscured by the attempt to manage the election. The tide of socialism was rising to an extent even larger than the outcomes of the 1922 election might suggest, and despite widespread Conservative-Coalition Liberal efforts to quell it with 'local arrangements', and a common desire for co-operation in the interests of 'respectable society'.

To understand the 1922 General Election it is necessary to focus on a number of different layers of understanding: what historians and political scientists have made of the election; what the party leaderships saw as the politically necessary and strategically sensible moves to be made in the aftermath of the crisis which had brought down the Lloyd George government in October 1922; how Conservatives and Liberals responded to divided parliamentary parties; how the Conservative leadership responded to press barons and party associations which often had very different imperatives from each other; and how candidates tried to negotiate the political landscapes within their own constituencies by giving promises, and by representing their politics in certain ways. It is the interaction between the Conservatives under Andrew Bonar Law and the Lloyd George Liberals (also variously known as the National Liberals and the Coalition Liberals) which is the primary focus of this study. The 1922 General Election was almost labyrinthine in its complexities and levels, making the kind of generalisation necessary for it to serve as a reliable datum point of the shifting sands of British politics as problematic as the 1918 Coupon Election. Never was a

British general election more deserving of the label 'it's complicated', and with political identities in flux never was it more true to say that a general election was, in reality, hundreds of separate local contests each peculiar to itself. In the consensus view of interwar British politics the 1922 General Election emerges as a comparatively quiet and uninteresting contest that heralded a short-lived and rather dull Conservative government that was the antithesis of the fireworks and drama of the Lloyd George years. For Robert Blake in 1955 it was clear that 'few elections in modern times have been fought in an atmosphere of greater confusion and obscurity than the General Election of 1922'.[1] Charles Loch Mowat commented in the same year: 'The campaign was quiet ... Issues of principle were ... glossed over'.[2] That was certainly true of the Conservative and Liberal parties, but less so in the case of Labour. Noteworthy largely for a number of breakthroughs by the Labour Party in urban centres, especially Glasgow, Manchester and Sheffield, the election suggested that Labour might be about to emerge as the second party of government in British politics. This consensus narrative formed in the 1970s, and it has not been seriously questioned since. And yet that period from around 1920 to 1924 remains central to the work of the historians of British political parties and the biographers of the 'big beasts' of interwar British politics. It was during this period that the Liberal-Conservative duopoly gave way to a battle between Labour and the Conservatives, and a political scene dominated by Stanley Baldwin and Ramsay MacDonald. As Chris Cook notes in his 'study of constituency politics and electoral change' from 1922 to 1929: 'Between the fall of the Lloyd George Coalition in 1922 and the General Election of October 1924 British politics was transformed'.[3] For David Powell that period was one of 'the most confused and disturbed in British political history' as a fundamental realignment of British politics took place.[4] Given the importance of this period the consensus narrative needs more careful evaluation because it obscures potential differences of emphasis, and subtleties of analysis that need to be understood and which do tie that election in with some of the big shifts happening within British politics during this period.

For historians of a Liberal Party, divided since 1916 between the adherents of Asquith and Lloyd George, the period following on from the 'dismal results'[5] of the election was marked by on-going decline fed by continuing personal rivalries and long-standing 'basic contradictions' about the nature and future of liberalism in the post-Victorian age.[6] The biographers of the leaders of the two wings of British Liberalism have expressed some mystification at the behaviour of the two men during the campaign. Kenneth Morgan argued in 1979 that: 'The National Liberals [under Lloyd George] fought a half-hearted and irrelevant campaign in 1922. Their leader was disengaged in mind'.[7] Martin Pugh almost a decade later went further in his concerns at Lloyd George's half-hearted campaigning: 'The 1922 election came too soon for Lloyd George to organise, or even decide what to say'.[8] For Trevor Wilson, in his study of the decline of the Liberal Party, the fall of the coalition and what followed were part of Lloyd George's pivotal role as the chief secondary factor, behind the First World War, in the downfall of that party.[9]

The behaviour of Asquith was perhaps even more inexplicable. As Stephen Koss notes, Asquith in 1922 decided to 'hedge his bets' by publicly leaving open the door to co-operation with the Conservatives after the election. His luncheon date, with Sir George Younger, the long-term chair of the Conservative Party organisation, in the midst of the campaign on 6 November caused great surprise and no little comment.[10] In 1922 British Liberalism seemed virtually rudderless despite the hands of both Lloyd George and Asquith on the party-political tiller. Even more surprisingly in 1922 Lloyd George, the one-man political dynamo who electrified British politics across the early decades of the twentieth century, appeared to have entirely spent his energies. The great ship of British Liberalism was going nowhere and would shortly be revealed to be in a sinking condition.

While the 1922 General Election was part of an era of decline for the Liberal Party, for the historians of the Conservative Party the era is characterised by a sense of rebirth as, in Maurice Cowling's view, the Conservative Party made a conscious decision about replacing the Liberals with the Labour Party as their principal rival.[11] For Robert Blake, victory in the 1922 campaign was part of a process of 'clambering back' from the wilderness that the party had been cast into following the 1906 general election.[12] And yet, as can be seen in Blake's *The Conservative Party from Peel to Churchill*, the circumstances in which the coalition had ended tend to catch the eye of the historian rather than the campaign which followed.[13] Nevertheless, at the outset of the election the omens for Conservative victory 'cannot have seemed good'.[14] The eventual victory of the Conservative Party under Andrew Bonar Law was therefore, in Blake's eyes, a 'personal triumph'[15] and in the opinion of R. J. Q. Adams, a vindication of Bonar Law's reluctant decision to guide the Conservatives back towards sustainable independence no matter what the personal cost.[16] His campaign, characterised, and in some cases dismissed, as 'tranquillity' was the perfectly pitched message following the hustle and bustle of the Lloyd George administration.[17] And yet, even in the midst of this quiet campaign Bonar Law was at one point suspected of 'cosying up to the Liberals' under Asquith.[18]

By contrast Labour historians have seen the 1922 General Election as a pivotal moment in Labour's drive to power: part of the inevitable political flowering of the growth of the wider labour/union movement, as Ross McKibbin sees it.[19] For Francis Williams writing in 1950, in the midst of the Attlee governments, the 1922 General Election was a vital test of how far Labour had come since 1918 with the Labour Party emerging from the election as a practically 'new party'.[20] Andrew Thorpe writing at the time of the dawn of the Blair government in 1997, almost fifty years after Williams, provided detail on the impact of the 1922 election on the Labour Party: 'By 1922 it had asserted its independence, was clearly the opposition to the Conservatives, had asserted the primacy of parliamentary over other methods of achieving change, and felt comfortable with policy and … had credibility on political issues'.[21] David Marquand, Ramsay MacDonald's biographer, confirms both the sense that Labour was hoping for much from the 1922 election and, in the event, they were not to be disappointed.[22] As David Thackeray has noted, the party which emerged from the 1922 General Election was very much MacDonald's Party.[23] The outcome of the election was a demonstration of the progress and strength of the Labour central organisation which complemented, in Worley's view, an otherwise multi-faceted Labour identity which could vary and adapt itself from constituency to constituency according to local socio-economic conditions and circumstances.[24]

Beyond the conundrums and differences of emphasis raised by the historians of the different political parties, and the biographers of the leading politicians, election specialist Michael Kinnear, who completed his thesis at Oxford on the 1922 General Election, noted a distinct change during the course of the campaign that was pivotal to its outcome:

> The election of 1922 fell into two distinct halves: Until nomination day, the parties recovered from the shock of the Carlton Club meeting, but a possible debate over the fall of the old coalition failed to develop. The electors had a brief period of repose after the tumult of the Lloyd George years, but in the second half of the campaign new issues appeared which knocked many voters out of their

> complacency. It can be argued that both the period of quiet confusion and of renewed strife were necessary to produce a Conservative majority in this election: The first showed the voters the contrast with the unsettled days of the coalition, and the second made them realise how precarious was their newly acquired peace.[25]

The further one drills down into the historiography of the 1922 General Election, the more subtle points and differences emerge, which suggest the need for a re-evaluation as we try to come to terms with its part in the transformations which mark British politics between 1918 and 1924.

The greater availability of private family papers, and the digitisation of many newspapers, facilitate that re-examination. Two of these 'new' private paper collections are particularly interesting. The papers of Lieutenant-Colonel G. J. S. Scovell, largely complete and within their original file structure, were acquired by the privately held Lloyd George Archive in 2016 following a house clearance and auction. From 1919 to 1922 he served as general secretary of the Coalition Liberal Party Organisation playing a critical role in the development of that party and its preparations for the 1922 General Election. Meanwhile the papers of Sir Leslie Wilson, Conservative chief whip in 1922, sat largely unknown and unused in the Fryer Library in the University of Queensland until their use by Luke Stanley in a 2019 article in *Parliamentary History*.[26] These sources, from figures close to the heart of events, but sufficiently minor to ensure that their papers were not subject to sanitisation or picking over by biographers official and unofficial, allow us to re-examine our understandings of the 1922 election which were formed several decades ago.

Let us first begin by examining the conventional narrative. Lloyd George resigned as prime minister on 19 October 1922, just three hours after Conservative MPs meeting at the Carlton Club voted to end the coalition government elected in the 1918 Coupon Election by 187 votes to 88, according to widely reported but incorrect accounts.[27] Returning to Downing Street after resigning, Lloyd George discussed his political options with three ex-Coalition Liberal ministers including H. A. L. Fisher and Alfred Mond. Despite their urging to come out openly as a Liberal, Lloyd George still wavered even as he prepared to make a previously arranged speech at Leeds on 21 October. The wavering and the advice from ex-ministers was interesting. Lloyd George had options in front of him: to declare as a Liberal and hope to achieve some sort of re-unification between the two wings of the party; to carry on with the Lloyd George (Coalition) Liberals which had emerged as a semi-separate splinter group from the main Liberal Party between 1916 and 1920; or perhaps to try and establish some new force in British politics, by reaching out to some of those Conservatives who had voted in favour of maintaining the coalition government at the Carlton Club meeting. In October 1922 several different paths lay before Lloyd George and the Coalition Liberals, and for that matter before their former Conservative Party partners.

On 20 October Lloyd George caught the train to the north of England from St Pancras Station making a series of speeches in some of the constituencies en route as he prepared to give a major speech at Leeds. As Michael Kinnear notes, each speech along the way seemed to herald a different position, evidence that even after his meeting with Liberal ministers Lloyd George simply did not know what strategy and tactics he should adopt for the forthcoming election, which seemed to be the inevitable outcome of the decision at the Carlton Club: 'During his tour on 20 October he moved from a modified acceptance of the situation at Bedford, in which he did not denounce those who had deposed him, to an appeal at Wellingborough for support against "a mere party game"'.[28] By the time he reached Sheffield, Lloyd George appeared ready to direct his oratory towards the Tory die-hards who had brought down the coalition. All was set for the big speech at Leeds which offered the former prime minister the perfect platform to define future policy and to launch his election campaign.

At Leeds, with the newspapers in attendance, the former prime minister's speech failed to ignite his followers or the campaign.[29] He had left St Pancras Station for the campaign trail northwards declaring: 'My sword is in my hand'.[30] By the end of the Leeds speech it appeared that he had managed to lose it before arriving at the venue. As the *Daily Herald* ran: 'Sword Left in Train: Mr. Ll. George Disappoints his Followers'.[31] The former prime minister spoke largely about his record in office and said absolutely nothing to suggest that he had clarified the future direction of the former Liberal coalitionists. It appeared that Lloyd George had lost his dynamism, and perhaps his political direction altogether. In the Leeds speech Bonar Law, who had led the attack on the continuance of the coalition at the Carlton Club meeting, was praised for his simplicity of approach and there was nothing to suggest that Lloyd George might be preparing for barnstorming attacks on the Conservative Party as a foretaste of the election that was yet to come. Chris Cook argues that the speech was Lloyd George effectively stalling for time, trying to evaluate the political options before committing himself and his party one way or the other.[32]

It was, however, somewhat surprising that Lloyd George would need to stall for time. The coalition government had been approaching its end since late 1921 as Lloyd George and Chamberlain considered bouncing the parties into a general election to renew the coalition. In December 1921 Sir Malcolm Fraser, the chief agent of the Conservative Party, had advised Austen Chamberlain in a report seen by Lloyd George that if both parties went to the country, in say February 1922, they would 'probably get back with a majority' but at the cost of splitting the Conservative Party 'from top to toe', such was the opposition to continued coalition.[33] Fraser considered that in the event of an election the number of Labour MPs was likely to increase and many of the Conservatives returned would do so as Independent Conservatives with little loyalty or affection for a Lloyd George government. Senior Conservatives, including Neville Chamberlain, Sir Percy Woodhouse and Sir Alex Leith, expressed their opposition to an election in early 1922.[34] Sir George Younger, the party chairman, felt forced to write to constituency chairs to advise them that, while the decision to seek an early election lay with the prime minister, in constitutional terms, Conservative Central Office was strongly against such a course.[35] Younger took to the press to campaign against such a move.[36] While Younger might suggest to the public and constituency chairs that there was no crisis, the sight of the chair of the Conservative Party openly campaigning against an election to maintain the coalition reassured no one. Chamberlain was in despair at being caught between parts of his own party and Lloyd George busy on the international stage at the Cannes conference.[37]

Forcing fusion between the new parties would negate the centrifugal forces at the heart of the coalition where each party blamed the other for key parts of government policy. The failure in early 1922 of a further attempt on the part of both the Coalition Liberals and the leadership of the Conservative Party to effect some form of fusion between the two parties underlined the growing instability of the coalition government. Events over the spring and summer of 1922, with the failure of the Cannes conference (6–13 January 1922), and the failure of the government's Near Eastern policy bringing the prospect of an Anglo-Turkish war, did nothing to revive the coalition's fortunes with voters and the members of the Conservative Party.

By early October, with headlines such as 'Ministry's Failing Credit' the signs had been unmistakeable that a large section of the Conservative Party wanted to end the coalition between the parties.[38] In the days before the Carlton Club meeting (made a three-line whip in the telegram to MPs from Leslie Wilson), a full-scale effort by the leaderships of both parties had been underway to try and rescue a deteriorating situation.[39] The looming Newport by-election,[40] which would be won by an Independent Conservative, together with the political fallout from the failure of Lloyd George's Near Eastern policy, had caused great excitement. The situation in Newport had suggested a breakdown in coalition arrangements with the Coalition Liberal Party organisation reportedly helping the independent Liberal candidate, and the local Conservative Association clamouring for Conservative Central Office to back the Independent Conservative.[41] Chamberlain had lamented this 'beautiful illustration of the results of a split' but conceded 'at every stage we are being forced further and further apart and it is difficult to see what the end will be'.[42] The press meanwhile had talked about the 'growing estrangement' between Conservatives and the coalition.[43] The national press had understandably highlighted 'General Election Signs' and had questioned the prospects for 'An Immediate Election'.[44] By 13 October Austen Chamberlain, as leader of the Conservative Party, had been forced to give a rallying-call speech in Birmingham in which he had called on all 'Constitutional and Conservative' parties to help defend the 'social and economic order'.[45] Senior Conservatives such as Lord Derby warned Chamberlain that while broad sections of the Conservative Party had no problem working with Coalition Liberals, distrust of the prime minister was making the continuance of the coalition incredibly difficult.[46] Chamberlain in response had raised the prospect that Lloyd George might voluntarily step down from the premiership in favour of a Conservative and worried that in any election in which the two parties did not fight as a coalition Labour might secure 200–250 seats.[47] His public and private attempts at reassuring the party had not been well received within the Conservative Party and *The Times* had reported that junior ministers were considering their position.[48] The profound sense that the coalition was about to break up had not been eased by a further rallying-call speech at Manchester by Lloyd George on 14 October.[49] Chamberlain knew that he was facing a revolt by Conservative junior ministers in the government and was privately conceding that his position as party leader was all but untenable.[50] By the eve of the Carlton Club meeting the betting was very firmly in favour of a rejection of the coalition with a split in the Conservative Party, and a general election the likely outcome.[51] The outcome of the Carlton Club meeting was deeply unsurprising, and Lloyd George's resignation as prime minister, just three hours after its conclusion, was further evidence of it. Thus, it would seem surprising that Lloyd George on 20 October, as he prepared to take the train and get on what had become the campaign trail, was not fully ready to put into action the political strategy that he had long had time to think about.

For whatever reason, the Lloyd George who made a series of speeches as he travelled north on 20 October was not the Lloyd George of old, or the Lloyd George that the crowds and press expected. This set a pattern for the entire election, with Lloyd George making a limited number of public appearances which failed to set the campaign trail alight. The campaign appeared half-hearted, with the party and its leader looking tired and largely bereft of ideas. It is unsurprising that Michael Kinnear should put this down to Lloyd George being worn out after six years as prime minister, and perhaps also out of a concern that in the past his aggressive oratory had sometimes produced misunderstandings and facilitated deliberate misrepresentations.[52] But as Kinnear also points out, Lloyd George was perhaps anxious to maintain good relations with the Conservative backbenchers, and we must ask why this might be so, and what it might suggest about Lloyd George's strategy. What also does it perhaps point to in terms of the Conservative Party?

Following the Carlton Club meeting on 19 October Lloyd George and his cabinet presented their resignations to King George V. Lloyd George advised the king to invite Bonar Law to form a ministry. At the 1918 general election the Conservatives had gained 379 seats in a 707-seat House of Commons. Setting aside the issue of the existence and demise of the coalition, the Conservatives were in a position to form a government of their own, and their parliamentary position had been further entrenched by Sinn Féin's boycott of Westminster, and the eventual removal of the majority of Irish seats from Westminster politics under the 1921 Irish settlement. Following Lloyd George's resignation King George V did indeed ask Bonar Law to form a ministry, which he delayed until 23 October, by which time he had been elected leader of the Conservative Party. Although the expectation was that Bonar Law would call an election there was no immediate requirement to do so. Indeed, there was widespread speculation that any election would be delayed until after final ratification of the Irish Bill, should there be opposition to it.[53] In the event there was none, but there was no absolute imperative to call an immediate election, and certainly not one as soon as 16 November 1922. Might Bonar Law then have had other reasons to hold an election so soon beyond allowing the country the chance to make its views known?

On the same day as Lloyd George made his Leeds speech, Lord Derby appealed to Lancashire Conservatives not to split the moderate vote by opposing the Lloyd George Liberals. The call to maintain a party truce between Coalition Liberals and Conservatives was echoed north of the border by the Scottish Conservatives who declared that they would not run candidates against their former colleagues in the coalition.[54] This was perhaps unsurprising. As the Oswestry MP William Bridgeman noted it was the Scottish Tory MPs who had most visibly been upset by the outcome of the Carlton Club meeting, fearing that they 'might lose their seats' at the next election as a result of the decision to end the coalition.[55] In response, the Scottish National Liberals declared that they would reciprocate the favour.[56] Conservative Central Office endorsed the arrangement, and had no objection to an equivalent party truce in Lancashire where similar concerns about the rise of Labour were prevalent. This developed into a wider endorsement by Conservative Central Office of those associations where they wished to maintain 'local arrangements' or pacts between Conservatives and Coalition Liberals. This championing of the rights of the associations to make their own arrangements was a strategic move, both in terms of a divided party and considerations about the likely outcome of the general election, that could be hidden behind the respect of the Central Party for the views of the members.

South of the border, despite some expression of support for local party pacts in areas such as Bristol, sitting Coalition Liberals appeared vulnerable, with a general sense of pessimism over the chances of a party that had only begun to take shape in 1920, as it was clear that Lloyd George and his followers were personae non gratae with the wider Liberal Party. In 1975 Chris Cook concluded that Lloyd George 'was powerless to prevent' the approaching debacle.[57] Echoing Kinnear's statements about Lloyd George's apparent inability after six long years in office to respond to the challenge of the 1922 General Election, Cook argues that the Coalition Liberal MPs were 'without a power base' and that Lloyd George was 'a leader with nothing to lead'.[58] Morgan concurs that Lloyd George 'cut a somewhat pathetic picture' and that the Coalition Liberal Party was really 'a disorganised affair'.[59] It was not, however, some sense of pessimism which dampened Lloyd George's political temper and his oratory on his journey to Leeds. He too could see both the danger from Labour, and

Conservative unease at what the 1922 General Election might bring. Local pacts were even more in the interest of the Coalition Liberal Party than the Conservatives in the interests of the fight against socialism.

If Lloyd George's campaign appearances lacked fire, then so too did those of the famously dour Bonar Law. In his speech on 23 October, as he became leader of the Conservative Party and took up the king's invitation to form a government, Bonar Law spoke warmly of Lloyd George's contribution to the postwar government. It was hardly the stuff of bitter party controversy. The general election campaign from this point lasted little more than three weeks and the first part of it until 2 November was marked by a period of comparative quiet, partly as a result of the parties having to get their constituency machines in order before the poll. Borough council elections also helped to suppress the exchanges between Liberals and Conservatives, both in terms of absorbing the attention of party activists at the local level, but also the need to maintain arrangements to keep Labour out of office. Although the campaign after this point was enlivened by a number of personal spats between senior figures, including one between Churchill and Curzon, and one between Lord Birkenhead and Leslie Wilson, there was a sense that personal animosities were filling the vacuum left by the absence of heated political debate about the future direction of the parties and the country. Moreover, the on-going threat of war with a resurgent nationalist Turkey acted as a further restraining influence on the cross-fire between Coalition Liberals and their former Conservative partners, although Beaverbrook's *Daily Express* used the situation in the Near East to castigate Coalition Liberals and their Conservative allies as 'War-Mongers', who had been willing to plunge the country into a further conflict to keep Lloyd George in office.[60]

In terms of the programmes put forward to the electorate there were comparatively few issues to really set the parties apart from one another, and between the Coalition Liberals and Conservatives there was a considerable amount of admiration expressed for each other's achievements in navigating the country through the war and the difficult period immediately thereafter. Although Bonar Law favoured the introduction of tariffs to safeguard staple industries, he made it clear that the question would have to wait for another election, and a fresh mandate.

Labour's proposal to introduce a capital levy to target those who had done well out of the war caused a reaction amongst middle-class voters. The public didn't understand it and had little enthusiasm for it, especially with the newspapers suggesting to the middle classes that it impinged on the interests of business.[61] There was some alarm in Labour circles at its reception, with clarifications being issued to candidates and agents during the campaign to help defuse it as an issue with the media and at public meetings.[62]

The outcome of the poll on 15 November came as a surprise. A clear Conservative majority, an increase in the Labour vote share and disappointment for the Asquithian and Lloyd George Liberals. After such a dull campaign there was widespread expectation that the eventual result would be inconclusive with perhaps a minority government emerging. The outcome was a clear victory for the Conservatives with the Labour Party emerging as His Majesty's Most Loyal Opposition.

The result for the Coalition Liberals, and the rival Asquithian Liberals, proved to be disastrous. British Liberalism had entered a decline which would not be arrested despite the re-unification of the two wings of liberalism in 1923, and Lloyd George's return to form as the firebrand of British politics after his seemingly atypical performance in 1922. In hindsight it appeared that only Bonar Law's charitable nature had saved the 'Coalie Libs' from almost total annihilation as they ran a lacklustre campaign under a tired leader.[63] However, was the lack of heat between the Conservatives and Coalition Liberals, and the limited evidence of on-going close working relationships between the two parties in some areas, really part of wider hopes to manage the outcome of the election? And, if so, why was this attempt at management so tentative as to result in an unexpected outcome in the general election, and to leave few traces for later historians to pick up on?

Table 0.1: Outcome of the 1922 General Election

Party	Votes	Share	Candidates	MPs	Unopposed
Conservative	5,502,298	38.5%	482	344	42
Liberal	2,668,143	18.9%	333	62	6
Co. Liberal	1,412,772	9.4%	144	53	4
Labour	4,237,439	29.7%	414	142	4
Communist	33,349	0.2%	5	1	–
Nationalist	112,528	0.5%	5	3	1
NDP[64]	52,233	0.4%	7	–	–
Others	373,370	2.4%	51	10	–
Total	14,392,330	100.00%	1,441	615	57

Notes

1 Robert Blake, *The Unknown Prime Minister: The Life and Times of Andrew Bonar Law 1858–1923* (London: Eyre and Spottiswoode, 1955), 468.

2 Charles Loch Mowat, *Britain Between the Wars* (London: Methuen, 1955), 145.

3 Chris Cook, *The Age of Alignment: Electoral Politics in Britain 1922–1929* (London: Macmillan, 1975), 3.

4 David Powell, *British Politics, 1910–35: The Crisis of the Party System* (London: Routledge, 2004), 117.

5 Paul Adelman, *The Decline of the Liberal Party, 1910–1931* (London: Routledge, 1995), 40.

6 Chris Cook, *A Short History of the Liberal Party 1900–1984* (Basingstoke: Macmillan, 1984), 83.

7 Kenneth O. Morgan, *Consensus and Disunity: The Lloyd George Coalition Government 1918–22* (Oxford: Clarendon Press, 1979), 358.

8 Martin Pugh, *Lloyd George* (London: Longman, 1988), 160.

9 Trevor Wilson, *The Downfall of the Liberal Party* (London: Collins, 1966), 244–59.

10 Stephen Koss, *Asquith* (London: Allen Lane, 1976), 257.

11 Maurice Cowling, *The Impact of Labour, 1920–1924: The Beginning of Modern British Politics* (Cambridge: Cambridge University Press, 1971), 1.

12 John Ramsden, *An Appetite for Power: A History of the Conservative Party Since 1830* (London: Harper Collins, 1998), 222–46.

13 Robert Blake, *The Conservative Party from Peel to Churchill* (London: Fontana, 1972), 209.

14 Blake, *The Unknown Prime Minister*, 464.

15 Blake, *The Unknown Prime Minister*, 474.

16 R. J. Q. Adams, *Bonar Law* (Stanford: Stanford University Press, 1999), 302 ff.

17 Blake, *The Unknown Prime Minister*, 466.

18 Blake, *The Unknown Prime Minister*, 465.

19 Ross McKibbin, *The Evolution of the Labour Party 1910–1924* (Oxford: Oxford University Press, 1974).

20 Francis Williams, *Fifty Years' March: The Rise of the Labour Party* (London: Odhams, 1950), 297.

21 Andrew Thorpe, *A History of the British Labour Party* (Basingstoke: Palgrave, 1997), 47.

22 David Marquand, *Ramsay MacDonald* (London: Jonathan Cape, 1977), 279, 283.

23 David Howell, *MacDonald's Party: Labour Identities and Crisis 1922–1931* (Oxford: Oxford University Press, 2002).

24 Matthew Worley, *The Foundations of the British Labour Party: Identities, Cultures and Perspectives 1900–39* (London: Routledge, 2016), 193–212.

25 Michael Kinnear, *The Fall of Lloyd George: The Political Crisis of 1922* (London: Macmillan, 1973), 155.

26 Luke Stanley, 'The Rebel Chief Whip: The Role of Leslie Wilson in the Fall of the Lloyd George Coalition, 1922', *Parliamentary History* 38, no. 2 (2019): 224–43.

27 'Mr Lloyd George Resigns the Premiership', *Daily Mirror*, 20 October 1922, 1. The actual result, as Kinnear notes, was 187 to 86 and this is confirmed in a telegram to Lord Berwick giving the result of the Carlton Club Meeting. Conservative and Unionist Association (Ludlow Division), Shropshire Archives, X112/21/5/9/2/3.

28 Kinnear, *The Fall of Lloyd George*, 155–6.

29 See Leeds Brief, October 1922, Lloyd George Papers (Parliamentary Archives) LG/F/254.

30 'Mr Lloyd George', *Yorkshire Evening Post*, 21 October 1922, 6.

31 'Sword Left in Train', *Daily Herald*, 23 October 1922, 1.

32 Cook, *Age of Alignment*, 16. See also Chris Cook and John Stevenson, *A History of British Elections Since 1689* (Routledge: London, 2014), 124.

33 Sir Malcolm Fraser to Chamberlain, 31 December 1921, Austen Chamberlain papers, Cadbury Research Library, Birmingham, AC32/4/1a.

34 Undated Notes by Mr Neville Chamberlain MP, Austen Chamberlain papers, Cadbury Research Library, AC32/4/7, Undated Notes by Sir Percy Woodhouse, Austen Chamberlain papers, Cadbury Research Library, AC32/4/10, Undated Notes by Sir Alex Leith, Austen Chamberlain papers, Cadbury Research Library, AC32/4/8.

35 Circular letter from Sir George Younger, 9 January 1922, Austen Chamberlain papers, Cadbury Research Library, AC32/4/14.

36 Diary of Younger's press campaign, Austen Chamberlain papers, Cadbury Research Library, AC32/4/15.

37 Chamberlain to Lloyd George, 12 January 1922, Austen Chamberlain papers, Cadbury Research Library, AC32/2/26.

38 'Ministry's Failing Credit', *The Times*, 10 October 1922, 10.

39 Note from Leslie Wilson, amplifying his telegram of 16 October 1922, Bull Papers 5/6, Churchill College Cambridge.

40 'Conservative Wins Newport', *The Daily Mirror*, 19 October 1922, 3.

41 Fraser to Chamberlain, 6 October 1922, Austen Chamberlain papers, Cadbury Research Library, AC32/3/31.

42 Chamberlain to Fraser, 6 October 1922, Austen Chamberlain papers, Cadbury Research Library, AC33/2/32.

43 'Premier's Future', *The Times*, 11 October 1922, 10, and 'The Premier's Dilemma', *The Times*, 13 October 1922, 12.

44 'The Coalition Crisis', *The Times*, 12 October 1922, 12, and 'The Premier's Dilemma', *The Times*, 13 October 1922, 12.

45 'A Chamberlain Apologia', *The Times*, 14 October 1922, 10.

46 Derby to Chamberlain, 10 October 1922, Austen Chamberlain papers, Cadbury Research Library, AC33/2/33.

47 Chamberlain to Parker Smith, 11 October 1922, Austen Chamberlain papers, Cadbury Research Library, AC32/2/38.

48 'Political Notes', *The Times*, 14 October 1922, 10.

49 'Mr Lloyd George's Speech', *The Times*, 16 October 1922, 12.

50 See Leslie Wilson to Chamberlain, 12 October 1922, Austen Chamberlain papers, Cadbury Research Library, AC33/2/43, Chamberlain to Birkenhead, 12 October 1922, Austen Chamberlain papers, Cadbury Research Library, AC33/2/45.

51 'The Crisis', *The Times*, 18 October 1922, 12.

52 Kinnear, *The Fall of Lloyd George*, 156.

53 'Fall of the Coalition', *The Times*, 12 October 1922, 12.

54 Kinnear, *The Fall of Lloyd George*, 157.

55 William Bridgeman to his eldest son, 21 October 1922, Bridgeman Papers, Shropshire Archives X4629/1/1922/21.

56 Cook, *The Age of Alignment*, 17.

57 Cook, *The Age of Alignment*, 17.

58 Cook, *The Age of Alignment*, 16.

59 Morgan, *Consensus and Disunity*, 358.

60 '"War-Mongers" in the Pillory', *The Daily Express*, 6 November 1922, 1.

61 See for example, Press Cuttings 26 and 27 October 1922, Labour Party Archive, LP/ELEC/1922/1.

62 See for example the clarification on the Capital Levy in *The Election News*, No. 1, 4 November 1922, 1, Labour Party Archive, LP/ELEC/1922/1.

63 Kenneth O. Morgan, 'Lloyd George's Stage Army: The Coalition Liberals, 1918–22', in *Lloyd George: Twelve Essays*, ed. A. J. P. Taylor (London: Hamilton, 1971), 250. See also Morgan, *Consensus and Disunity*, 358.

64 National Democratic Party

Chapter 1

The party political outlook in October 1918

If Lloyd George's actions following the Carlton Club meeting and the apparent lack of direction and clarity in his public pronouncements during the last ten days of October smacked of indecision then it was scarcely surprising. The passing of the coalition might have been unlamented, but in political terms it had at least been a well-established feature of the political landscape and few could predict what would replace it. Since the turn of the century British politics had appeared to be in a state of flux. The Conservative Party had experienced a stunning defeat in the 1906 General Election, losing 246 seats in a landslide in favour of the Liberal Party under Sir Henry Campbell-Bannerman, which had won 397 seats, allowing it to form a government. The new Liberal government had embraced radical reform that antagonised the Conservative Party, creating serious political divisions over issues such as the demands of Irish nationalists for independence or at least home rule. The January 1910 General Election had resulted in a hung parliament as did the election in December 1910. The political deadlock had continued until the outbreak of war in 1914 which had, at least for the moment, restored a sense of national unity as the Liberals and Conservatives supported the war effort. The outbreak of war had also damaged the Labour Party, founded in 1900. It had grown out of a number of socialist parties and the trades union movement to return forty-two MPs in January 1910 and forty in December 1910. In 1914 the Labour Party was split between pacifists and those willing to support the war, and that raised questions about what would happen to the party in the long term.

In May 1915 unease at the lack of success on the battlefield forced Liberal prime minister Herbert Henry Asquith to re-organise his cabinet, admitting a number of leading Conservatives as ministers to form a coalition government. That arrangement had broken down in December 1916 as the Conservatives had conspired with David Lloyd George, the Liberal Secretary of State for War, to wrest significant power out of the hands of Asquith, who was seen as failing to prosecute the war, and the business of government, effectively. Rather than become a largely figurehead prime minister, Asquith had preferred to resign, leaving Lloyd George as prime minister, backed by Conservatives and a significant number of Liberal MPs. The coalition which Lloyd George oversaw had prosecuted the war to a conclusion but with the collapse of the German armies in late 1918 many wondered what might happen in terms of Britain's political future.

Both Labour and the rump of the Liberals, still under Asquith, appeared weak. The Conservatives appeared united, but had no wish to dispense with the services of Lloyd George, popularly referred to as the man who had won the war. He was too much of a vote winner. Lloyd George and his Liberal adherents had no wish to rejoin the Asquithian Liberals and Labour was yet another small party. Thus, a deal to extend the coalition into the peace had been rapidly hatched between the Lloyd George Liberals and the Conservatives. This had involved a letter of recognition (referred to as the coupon) being given to sitting MPs, whether Liberal or Conservative, who backed the continuation of the coalition into the peace.[1] Lloyd George's Liberal supporters had campaigned for sitting Conservatives and vice versa depending on the party affiliation of the sitting MP. It was a remarkable success and instead of a hung parliament the coalition of Conservatives and Lloyd George Liberals had won by a landslide with a mandate to address the problems of the peace. The election also marked a changing of the guard in political terms as the new parliament contained a large number of people without previous Westminster experience.[2] The end of the coalition in October 1922 re-opened the lingering questions about the future of the parties in the British political system. Were the Conservatives capable of gaining a majority in their own right? What might Lloyd George and his adherents do: seek re-unification with the rest of the Liberal Party under Asquith (reduced to just thirty-six MPs in 1918), join Labour (fifty-seven MPs in 1918), or try to form some kind of new party? Equally, what might Asquith attempt to do, and was the Labour Party capable of capitalising on the social and economic problems of postwar Britain to effect some form of political breakthrough, to match its progress in local elections since the end of the war? The questions were numerous, significant and far reaching. With Liberalism divided, the Conservatives unsure of themselves and split by the outcome of the Carlton Club meeting, and with Labour fighting to break through, the outcome of the 1922 General Election was a political roll of the dice, the outcome of which was anyone's guess.

There were other complicating factors that meant that the outcome of the election was unpredictable, which only added to the difficulties of strategy-makers within the parties. As Frank Owen commented, the outcome of the Carlton Club meeting meant that the coast was clear for a return to party politics but 'the coast was oddly be-fogged, and the course for any ship uncertain'.[3] In 1918 the electoral map had been redrawn (the largest exercise of its kind since 1885 to take account of the rapid growth in population of many areas). It was widely assumed that the redistribution would benefit the Conservatives, but the nature of the Coupon Election of 1918 meant that the impact of the new political landscape of the United Kingdom was still largely a matter of guesswork.

Within the constituencies the changing social and economic base of British politics with the rise of new voters, the postwar slump and decline of stable industries heightened the uncertainties while apparently increasing the opportunities for the left. The 1918 Representation of the People Act gave the vote not just to most women over thirty, but also brought in large numbers of new male voters as it enshrined the principle of universal male suffrage for those over twenty-one, and gave the vote to men aged nineteen and above who had fought in the war. The new provisions meant that the electorate had almost tripled between December 1910 and 1918 from 7,709,981 to 21,392,322. However, in 1918 many of them hadn't been able to vote as a result of problems with voter registration and the fact that many soldiers were still away serving overseas. Turnout was just 57.2 per cent. Just how this new electorate would vote was deeply uncertain.

With a strong Labour showing in local elections, and in by-elections after 1918, it appeared unlikely that either the Conservatives or the Liberals would be in a position to make the kind of gains to give them a majority in late 1922 which meant that renewed coalition or co-operation in some form was the most likely outcome of the election. Stopping socialism, rather than progressing Liberalism or Conservatism, was the imperative for many on the centre and right of British politics in 1920–22. Following the Carlton Club meeting, most pundits regarded a hung parliament as a racing certainty for the outcome of the 1922 General Election. As the London Correspondent of the *Gloucester Citizen* commented:

> Predictions of the future development of parties are obviously of little use until the General Election is over, and there never has been an election at which there was so great a difficulty in estimating the probable result. That any party will have a clear majority over all other parties I do not think anybody believes.[4]

It is unsurprising that most historians have concluded, like Kinnear, that: 'In 1922 most politicians regarded coalition as a natural mode of governing and they did not change their minds when the Carlton Club Meeting overthrew Lloyd George ... [;] far from damaging the long-term prospects for coalition, the meeting actually made such prospects more likely'.[5] In October 1922 many politicians on the centre right were convinced that with the divisions in the Conservative and Liberal Parties only some new 'arrangement' could save the country from the prospect of a Labour government. Philip Kerr, who had served as Private Secretary to Lloyd George from 1916 to 1921 expressed the worry of many when he wrote to his mother: 'I suppose Labour will come back with a majority, unless some new coalition, or some electoral agreement is reached'.[6]

If there was a reluctant acceptance amongst the politicians that a 'new coalition' or 'electoral agreement' might be necessary to prevent a Labour government then that, in the midst of an election campaign, was a difficult proposition to potentially sell to the electorate. It was an even harder task to get Conservative Party activists to accept it, especially in those constituencies where socialism was not considered an immediate threat. Many Conservative Associations, antagonised by Lloyd George's 'antics' and a perception that they were propping up the Coalition Liberals at the national level, had grown increasingly restive during the coalition. At a meeting of Conservative ministers on 26 July 1922 attended by both the party chairman and the chief whip it was reported that:

> the Central Office was being placed in very grave difficulty owing to the growing feeling of antagonism to the Coalition, as at present constituted, in the constituencies; and more especially, to the determination in many places, where Coalition Liberals sit, to put up Unionist candidates in opposition to these gentlemen at the next Election.[7]

The phrase 'as at present constituted' was tacit acceptance that while the premiership of David Lloyd George was increasingly toxic, the door to continued coalition, under some other leader, was certainly not closed. The practical outcome of this meeting was to be significant in the circumstances of the 1922 General Election. While it was agreed that Central Office could not fail to aid prospective parliamentary candidates properly selected by the Associations: 'they would continue to discourage contests in seats held by Coalitionists, so long as the Coalition lasted, and that official recognition would not be given to any candidate adopted under such circumstances'.[8]

After the Carlton Club meeting, however, how could a leadership dismissed as a 'Second XI' by former coalitionist Conservatives galvanise a divided party to fight a general election when the likely outcome was either a Labour government or a return to hated coalition. The former was unthinkable and the latter was the kind of practical political outcome which those who had brought down the coalition could scarcely discuss, let alone advocate publicly. The nuance in public debate about the future of the coalition had disappeared in September and October 1922. 'Coalition' in the approach to the 1922 General Election was 'the love that dare not speak its name'.[9] The party leadership could, however, stand by existing local arrangements and the decision of Conservative ministers 'to discourage contests in seats held by Coalitionists' and to refuse recognition and aid to any 'Conservative' candidate not properly selected in the usual way by their local association. Interestingly, the snap nature of the 1922 contest meant that there was very little time for such properly selected candidates to properly emerge. Perhaps this provides some explanation for the rush to the polls in unseemly haste after the Carlton Club meeting?

Most historians of the period have taken it for granted that Bonar Law, the man whose intervention at the Carlton Club meeting was pivotal in bringing down the coalition, was opposed to the very principal of coalition, but this overlooks some contemporary evidence that suggests that he may have not regarded coalition as a wholly dead possibility.[10] For one thing, Bonar Law had been the man in 1918 who had helped to broker the continuation of the wartime coalition into the peace. Maynard Colchester Weymss, stalwart of the Forest of Dean Conservative Association, noted on 24 October on the impending election and Bonar Law's assumption of the premiership: 'He is an out and out Conservative, but how far he is still a Coalitionist is impossible yet to say; I doubt whether he knows himself, at any rate in a speech he made yesterday to his constituents in Glasgow he said words to the effect that at present no one including himself, knew exactly where they are'.[11] The observation is noteworthy even if it can be partly offset by the fact that with the Forest of Dean held by Labour since 1918, Weymss was hoping for a united front between Conservatives and Coalition Liberals to get Labour out.[12] Whatever the local influences on the observation of Weymss as to Bonar Law's attitudes towards coalition, the same question mark must have been in the minds of other Conservatives as they surveyed the political landscapes just after the fall of the coalition. Those suspicions would have been further fuelled in 1922 when the Bonar Law of pre-war days (renowned for the savagery and force of his rhetoric against the Liberals)[13] seemed almost meek in his references to Lloyd George, even if allowances could be made for advancing age, illness and the impact of the loss of his wife in 1909 and two sons during the First World War.

In their calculations about the election the Conservatives also had to consider the potential difficulties which would arise if there was some new realignment on the centre-left of British politics that might see the emergence of a credible potential opposition to Conservative rule. Lloyd George might abhor socialism but Conservatives could not entirely rule out the possibility that the man who had overseen the people's budget in 1909–10, and for whom power held a magical attraction, might not make some arrangement with Labour and other 'progressive' elements against 'the forces of reaction'. Veteran Conservative Maynard Weymss in Gloucestershire expressed his concerns on 24 October about the dangers of Lloyd George forming a new party on the left of British politics: 'he would be a most powerful opponent if he decided to raise a Party in Opposition to Bonar Law … I most earnestly hope for the sake of the country, & for his own sake that he will not do this'.[14] The worry was undoubtedly underpinned by an outpouring of loathing for Lloyd George from many Asquithian Liberals. Public vilification of Lloyd George by the Asquithians suggested that a deal with Labour might be an easier proposition than the task of Liberal re-unification. As Liberal Grandee Lord Crewe commented in a speech soon after the break-up of the coalition, it was not 'possible to reunite with Mr Lloyd George and members of his late Government merely on the basis of a few Liberal phrases and some abuse on the part of the Carlton Club'.[15]

It was also difficult for many politicians to think in ways which were overtly along party-political lines. Many of those elected in 1918 were new MPs without a grounding in the pre-war adversarial politics of home rule for Ireland and the People's Budget. Conservatives and Coalition Liberals came from the same social strata. Many were friends as well as political allies: their diaries and letters detail the kind of social engagements and friendships that underpinned the politics of coalition. During the war the rhetoric of party had given way to the rhetoric of 'the national interest', 'England', 'for Britain' and 'the nation'. The coalition had survived for four years despite considerable grumbling and unhappiness because it was perceived as still being 'in the national interest'. Its opponents had only succeeded in breaking the bulk of the Unionist Party away from the coalition when foreign policy blunders had led to a renewed danger of war with Turkey. That possible war, and the foreign policy that went with it, were personally associated with Lloyd George. A Turkish war was perceived to be wholly against the public interest, although potentially very much in the favour of those who wished to maintain the coalition: a political trick to use the danger of war to reinforce the position of the prime minister over his colleagues and the parties. Given the legacies of 1914–18 this was unforgiveable. Lloyd George's willingness to risk war, in the interest of solidifying the coalition, was what had finally broken the parties apart.

This process by which the majority of the parliamentary Conservative Party distanced itself from the coalition and then finally broke with it does, however, require more detail and nuance than is common in most analyses where 'Lloyd George', 'the coalition' and 'the Coalition Liberals' are used as semi-interchangeable terms. The principal problem for most Conservatives, and Conservative MPs in particular, was Lloyd George. The Welsh wizard became their bête noire, obsessing and possessing party members in equal measure. In the spring and summer of 1922 many Conservative MPs were willing to continue with the coalition so long as it was under a Conservative prime minister.[16] Indeed, Lloyd George recognised the fact when in February 1922 he offered to step down as prime minister: a politically astute move which Chamberlain's sense of morality and loyalty would not allow him to accept. That offer, and the idea that Lloyd George might step down after a general election, effectively remained on the table during the last months of the coalition. This was evident on 26 July 1922, in a meeting between Chamberlain and senior Conservative ministers. A memorandum drawn up following the meeting noted that Leslie Wilson (chief whip) and George Younger (chair of the party):

> took exactly the same view as to the necessity for terminating the present Coalition at the end of this Parliament, and if possible, making an arrangement which would maintain the continuance of the rapprochement between the rank and file, between the Unionist and Co-Liberal Parties; and that they both believed the Unionist Party would be consolidated if a Leader of that political complexion were at the head of the Government. If they were assured that the attitude of the Prime Minister to a change was a benevolent one, it was obviously their opinion that such an offer ought not to be disregarded, and that it offered a solution of the present difficulties which, in their view, was the only one which would reasonably ensure a joint victory when an appeal is next made to the constituencies.[17]

This sense that the coalition should continue but that Lloyd George needed to be eased out maintained the uneasy relationship between the Conservatives and Coalition Liberals during the Summer and Autumn of 1922, and it was only the sense that Lloyd George might not be prepared to step aside and that he would use his influence over senior Conservatives like Chamberlain, and even run the risk of war to engineer a khaki Coupon Election, that finally brought down the government.

As late as 6 October Lord Derby, the Grandee of Lancashire Conservatism, could be found talking to Leslie Wilson, the chief whip, to advise him that the coalition could not be maintained without splitting the party, but that a good working relationship with the Coalition Liberals was essential if they were not to let in Labour at the next general election.[18] The electoral reliance in any general election of the Conservative Party on the Coalition Liberals was highlighted four days later in a meeting of senior Conservatives in the dining room of No.11 Downing Street.[19] Polling by the party indicated that in an election Labour would gain 200–250 seats, the Asquithians 50, the Lloyd George Liberals 50, with the rest being Conservative in a house of 615 members. The October prediction provides an interesting comparison with that which had been suggested in December by Sir Malcolm Fraser, the Principal Agent of the Conservative Party, who had suggested that an election in early 1922 would likely have returned 306 Conservative MPs and 96 Coalition Liberal MPs.[20] The figures suggested that the electoral stock of the Coalition Liberals was falling fast, and that the outcome of any election was on a knife edge with a coalition (Con-Lib or Lab-Lib) the most likely outcome. Chamberlain was convinced that 'no Government after the election could be formed without some sort of Coalition'.[21] Chamberlain was convinced of the necessity of remaining on good terms with the Coalition Liberals. The possibility that Lloyd George might be invited to retire was raised (probably by Younger and Wilson) but both Chamberlain and Balfour could not, in the name of honour, consider such a move. This prompted discussion of a second set of party figures which suggested that if the Conservatives went into an election on their own Labour would be secure around 150 seats, the Coalition Liberals 50 and the Asquithian Liberals around 70. This would leave the way clear to a small but workable Conservative majority. Chamberlain, Robert Horne, the Chancellor of the Exchequer, and Lord Birkenhead, the Lord Chancellor, each took strong exception to the figures. The split within the upper echelons of Conservative leadership, never mind within the wider party, was evident.

Chamberlain was dismayed at the division within the party and the prospect of having to tell Lloyd George to retire. The chief whip, Leslie Wilson, was similarly perturbed by the unwillingness of key members of the party hierarchy to dispense with Lloyd George's services. He was not the only one. Party chairman George Younger was deeply troubled at what he considered to be the loyalty, bordering on fanaticism, on the part of some Conservatives.[22] It was this sense that Lloyd George held sway over senior Conservatives to the detriment of the party that really animated Younger. As Michael Kinnear has noted, Younger was a man of Conservative principles rather than a fixed platform and his one abiding goal was 'party survival'.[23] Thus on 11 October Younger, Wilson and Sir Malcolm Fraser, Principal Agent of the Party (all of whom had been at the meeting with Chamberlain on the day before) went to see Bonar Law the ex-leader of the party in a 'private capacity'.[24] Their purpose was to sound out Bonar Law about the dangers facing the party and to encourage him to come forward as an alternative leader if Chamberlain refused to see sense.

With a crunch fast approaching, in the form of the meeting at the Carlton Club, Wilson on the 12 October found Chamberlain dejected but committed to a course of standing by Lloyd George.[25] Four days later he met him again to report that they were 'receiving numberless resolutions from Constituency Associations, Provincial Divisions, Clubs, and other Conservative bodies' against the continuation of the coalition.[26] Officials were resigning from the party, members cancelling their subscriptions and 184 Conservative MPs looked likely to stand as independent Conservatives at the next election if the coalition was maintained. For Wilson the party was on the verge of breaking up and he made this plain to Chamberlain. Wilson advised Chamberlain to end the coalition and:

> go to the country much on the lines of the Conservatives and the Liberal Unionists, that if we came back with a majority, a Government should be formed under a Conservative Prime Minister with such Coalition-Liberal Ministers as would serve under him. It appeared to be fully agreed all round that it was undesirable to alienate the Coalition-Liberal sympathisers and supporters generally, if this were possible.[27]

When the break came at the Carlton Club it was with Lloyd George, and the Conservatives under his sway, that the Conservative backbenchers broke with, rather than the idea of working with the Liberal Coalitionists. By the late summer of 1922 a majority of Conservative backbenchers considered that Lloyd George was bad for the country, but also bad for their party with his malign influence over the party leadership. The sense of desperation with the leadership eroded loyalties to Chamberlain in the midst of the Anglo-Turkish crisis. As William Bridgeman, Conservative MP and Minister for Mines, wrote to his mother a few days before the Carlton Club meeting, Chamberlain 'seems infatuated with Ll. G. and an unselfish desire to sacrifice himself (and us) to his devotion'.[28] The issue with the coalition was the issue of Lloyd George rather than coalition with the Liberals *per se*. In their complaints against the government Conservative politicians tended to be very specific in their concerns. As Bridgeman explained to his mother: 'We cannot go to an election as Members of a government asking for another term of office under L.G. It is his foreign policy which upsets me'.[29] Lloyd George had to go at all costs.

However, this did not prevent a sense of 'the national interest' colouring the rhetoric and thought of many within the Conservative Party even amongst its veterans. While the danger of war might trump all other considerations in terms of attitudes towards the Lloyd George coalition, in domestic policy the danger of Labour and the need to shut out the socialists was the very embodiment of the national interest for both Conservatives and many Liberals. This sentiment, with the implication that Conservatives and Lloyd George Liberals should continue to work together in the national interest, found considerable expression at the Carlton Club meeting and it was to do so thereafter.

Support for the idea of continued coalition, in some form or other, continued to be openly expressed in Conservative ranks after the meeting at the Carlton Club threw out Lloyd George along with the coalition, and this has rather been overshadowed by the actions of the diehards in the consensus narrative on the history of the Conservative Party. The diehard wing of the party with Lord Salisbury at its heart was energetic and open in their efforts to bring down the coalition in October 1922. On 17 October Salisbury held a meeting for over one hundred Conservative parliamentarians at 21 Arlington Street that had been fully reported in the press, in particular Lord Salisbury's denunciation of Lloyd George as a man whose 'convictions were not Conservative', who had not 'the same respect for tradition and [who] did not understand the immense importance which they attributed to the maintenance of law and order and the reasonable administration of finance, with regard to the due capacity of the country'.[30]

It was not surprising that in the aftermath of the Carlton Club meeting there were some like Hugh Cecil, Salisbury's brother and veteran Conservative Member for Oxford University, who saw the overthrow of Lloyd George as 'cast[ing] out Satan', with their sole aim afterwards of securing a Unionist majority, but there were many others who were only too happy to continue working with Lloyd George Liberals.[31] Robert Blake, pointing to the very strong support at the Carlton Club meeting for continued coalition, questioned in the 1970s:

> The real problem is not why 185 members voted against the coalition on October 19, 1922 ... but why the minority of 88 voted for it. Historians have not looked closely at this side of the question. What, in other words, was the motive force behind the Conservative coalitionists?[32]

Undoubtedly, Lord Blake is correct in his assumption that it was the desire to stop socialism, which for some Conservative members trumped narrow party interests. That significant minority played a now overlooked role the day before the Carlton Club meeting, in trying to push the idea that the party should remain in the coalition, that an immediate general election be called, and that then, when the electoral map of postwar Britain was clearer, the party could vote on whether or not to continue the coalition.[33] For many within Conservative ranks an election in late 1922 just might hand the country over to the Bolshevists. This was the principal theme in defence of 'honest co-operation' underlying the pro-coalition voices at the Carlton Club meeting including Austen Chamberlain, as party leader, and Arthur Balfour, as respected elder statesman and former prime minister.[34] The strength of pro-coalition feeling within the Conservative Party in the lead up to the rupture of the coalition must have been duly noted by Lloyd George and others within Coalition Liberal ranks.

If they did not notice the strength of continued support for the coalition within Conservative ranks before the Carlton Club meeting then it was certainly much in evidence after it. That support, combined with the split in Conservative ranks caused some Conservatives who had been supportive of Lloyd George to be careful in their pronouncements. Some dissident Coalition Conservatives, meanwhile, were courted by fellow Conservatives and members of their associations. For example, Sir William Bull (MP for Hammersmith South), received a letter from a fellow Conservative asking him to support Bonar Law and reassuring him that the prime minister was very eager to include in any future administration those Conservatives who had voted in favour of the continuance of the coalition at the Carlton Club meeting.[35] Scottish Conservative, John Gilmour (Glasgow Pollok),was similarly courted by Bonar Law with the offer of the post of Secretary of State for Scotland.[36] Gilmour, however, was not about to let ambition get in the way of his principles. He wrote to his constituency chairman that he was not prepared to accept office if that meant having to accept an end to all possibility of co-operation with the Coalition Liberals and their leader.[37]

Expressions of support within the party for the principle of coalition were often combined with public endorsements of Bonar Law that amounted to a declaration of loyalty to the leadership and a marker in favour of continued co-operation: both principle and practical politics carefully combined to leave the options open for members defending their seats and their political futures. In some cases, the declarations of support in favour of continued co-operation were clear and unequivocal. Sir Leslie Scott, Conservative MP for Liverpool Exchange, issued an election manifesto, with the encouragement of F. E. Smith, the pro-Lloyd George former Conservative Lord Chancellor, that pulled no punches:

> **Resignation**
> You returned me last March as a Conservative [as he faced a by-election on his appointment as Solicitor General] and a supporter of the alliance between moderate men of the Conservative and Liberal

> Parties. At a meeting of Conservative Ministers and Members of Parliament a resolution was carried in favour of separation. I could not in conscience retain my office and suddenly abandon those who have worked with us so long. I resigned my office.
>
> **A Conservative**
> But I am not less a Conservative. Having resigned my office, I can in conscience accept the decision of the party; and I am prepared to support Mr. Bonar Law in the belief that his Government will tackle the problems of the day in a moderate and reasonable spirit, and with a firm hand. I want to see the Conservative Party pull together. But when a Liberal agrees with me in principle I decline to treat him as an enemy.[38]

Supporters of the coalition within Conservative ranks co-operated with each to encourage support for the continuation of a close working relationship with the Lloyd George Liberals, and to voice that support in a variety of open and coded forms. For example, Robert Horne, coalition dissident and former chancellor of the exchequer, prepared an appeal to the electorate (which was scrutinised by a number of fellow dissidents in draft form). In the draft he carefully set out that while he remained convinced of the significance of working with Lloyd George in the interests of anti-socialism, if the outcome of the general election was a Conservative government then he would be only too happy to support Bonar Law.[39] Within the Conservative Party the Coalitionists were the object of some suspicion and derision, with Horne finding himself the target of a poem deriding him for being a 'diehard' Conservative supporter of the coalition.[40]

Other, less high-profile Conservative sympathisers with the old coalition, expressed their views in more coded forms. For example, Sir Harry Hope, veteran Scottish Conservative MP explained to his Constituency Association at Stirling on 21 October:

> The Unionist Party had always looked at the welfare of the State before that of party ... During the war the Unionist Party did all that it could in the national interest: it acted in no party spirit ... The Unionist party had not in front of them a party policy. Their task at the present time – and their leaders had realised it – was not to work for their party but to work for the country's good, and with those many problems still unsolved he was perfectly sure that Unionists

> would welcome the support of moderate opinion, so that they could walk steadily forward, solving problems as they came before them.[41]

This was followed by Lord Derby at Manchester making his appeal to Lancashire Conservatives not to engage in fratricidal strife with the Lloyd George Liberals. He said: 'Although Conservatives and Coalition Liberals did not go along the same roads they should march along parallel roads. There should be co-operation, but not coalition. Unionists recognised all that Mr Lloyd George had done and were determined to give him fair play'.[42] Throughout the party, and all the way to polling day, there were repeated expressions of support for coalitionism.

Even in safe Conservative seats further south, well away from the urban and industrial centres in Scotland, the north and South Wales, where the Labour Party was pressing the established parties hard, candidates could be found making warm noises about Mr Lloyd George and the possibility of continuing good working relationships. In Taunton on 21 October, Sir Arthur Griffith Boscawen, Minister for Agriculture under Lloyd George, but supporter of Bonar Law at the Carlton Club meeting, was happy to suggest: 'The Coalition was necessary during the war and the years which immediately followed, and he still hoped for co-operation with the Coalition Liberals with whom on most questions there was no quarrel'.[43] To the east, as far afield as Kent, public expressions of support for the coalition were evident. Moore-Brabazon (Chatham) and Hohler (Gillingham) both spoke warmly about the coalition during the campaign, with Hohler stating that he still favoured its continuation.[44] While Moore-Brabazon probably had an eye on drawing to him Coalition Liberal votes in order to defeat a strong Asquithian Liberal challenger, Hohler was under no such pressure. For electoral advantage, or as expressions of genuine sympathy for the idea of continued coalition, there was no mistaking that 'coalitionism' remained important in the thinking of many Conservative hopefuls in 1922.

If the party leaders thought that some new arrangement was the most likely outcome of the election, with the tide of die-hardism perhaps turned back by some Labour gains, then best not to make 'honest co-operation' after the election more difficult through a heated campaign. Perhaps best to avoid clear political separation between the platforms of both parties, and to maintain in many constituencies the harmonious relationships between Conservatives and Lloyd George Liberals. Diehard Tories in the south of

England might have little to fear from Labour, but in the Midlands, industrial north and Scotland it was a different picture. Keeping Labour out of the townhalls had become an imperative and one that 'die-hardism' elsewhere in the party and on the Conservative backbenches at Westminster imperilled. The situation invited local constituency associations to take rather a dim view of the shenanigans of MPs at the Carlton Club meeting, even though Bonar Law remained a figure of great respect.

Bonar Law in turn must have been only too aware of the feelings amongst some parts of the Tory grassroots, aware of the need not to split the anti-socialist vote, and to leave open the door to future co-operation, especially with Lloyd George privately talking up the chances of a sizeable number of Coalition Liberals being returned at the election.[45] As the *Hull Daily Mail* commented on Bonar Law's re-emergence as leader of the Conservative Party: 'There's a strong strain of bold obstinacy in the new Premier-elect of Scottish-Canadian composition, and the main consideration with everybody now is the solidarity of the Unionist Party'.[46] With the party already divided at Westminster between those who had supported the coalition at the Carlton Club meeting, and those, like Samuel Hoare, who were against further co-operation at almost any price, the last thing Bonar Law wanted was to have the divisions extend down to constituency level, between die-hards and those prepared to work with others in the interests of shutting out Labour in the forthcoming election. In terms of framing policy for the forthcoming election, Bonar Law's task, in trying not to exacerbate divisions, solidify the party/electoral base and leave open the door to post-poll co-operation, was horrendously difficult. A certain constructive ambiguity, of devolving issues to the level of individual associations, and of continuing to rely on already agreed 'local arrangements', as well as having a campaign of very short duration offered the best possible way forward in such confused circumstances.

Bonar Law's task had been eased considerably on 20 October, the day before Lloyd George's Leeds speech, by the conclusions of the group of senior Conservatives that he had entrusted, in the aftermath of the Carlton Club meeting, with the task of framing a platform for the election. The group consisting of Curzon, Derby, Amery, Lord Cave and Douglas Hogg, argued that the election should be fought almost exclusively on the grounds of a change of government with a fresh approach and fresh leadership.[47] Conveniently, and perhaps not unexpectedly, tariff reform as a traditional, if divisive, Conservative policy was to be left off the agenda, at least for now.

It was, perhaps, almost a relief to Bonar Law that the Scottish Conservatives, and then the Lancashire Conservatives, came forward to press for the continuation of local arrangements of co-operation with the Lloyd George Liberals. Responsiveness to the local grass-roots (with Lancashire a bastion of 'Free Trade' sentiment and Scottish Conservatives fearful of radical socialism)[48] was a useful position to hold in terms of the politics of a divided party, useful in terms of trying to shut out Labour, and useful in terms of potentially maximising the number of Conservative MPs returned at the election. The Conservatives had been the dominant block in the coalition at Westminster, and they would have most to lose from three- or four-way fights involving Liberals (Asquith and Lloyd George) and Labour. It was also useful in terms of fighting the local elections and in building some potential bridges for future co-operation with the Lloyd George Liberals. There would be those, however, who tried to rock the boat of co-ordination and try to trigger significantly greater levels of exchange between Conservatives and Coalition Liberals.

For example, in Scotland the *Sunday Post* on 22 October attacked MPs of all parties for failing to deliver the economies promised in 1918. It called on electors to challenge associations if they tried to put forward for re-election those MPs who had failed to ease the financial burden on the nation and on the taxpayer: 'If the bulk of the present MPs are welcomed by the Associations, then it is the bounden duty of the electors to set up rival candidates in every constituency'.[49] Right from the outset, the policy of constructive ambiguity, and letting local arrangements stand, was under pressure and that pressure would intensify during the campaign.

Notes

1 See Roy Douglas, 'The Background to the "Coupon" Election Arrangements', *English Historical Review* 86 (1971): 318–36.

2 See John M. McEwen, 'The Coupon Election of 1918 and Unionist Members of Parliament', *Journal of Modern History* 34, no. 3 (1962): 294–306 (299).

3 Frank Owen, *Tempestuous Journey: Lloyd George, His Life and Times* (London: Hutchinson,1954), 660.

4 'Our London Letter', *Gloucester Citizen*, 23 October 1922, 5.

5 Kinnear, *The Fall of Lloyd George*, 2.

6 Philip Kerr to his mother, 25 October 1922, 11th Marquess of Lothian Papers, National Records of Scotland GD40/17/467/28.

7 Sir George Younger 'Meeting of the Unionist Members of the Cabinet, Wednesday, 26th July 1922', Wilson Papers, Fryer Library, MSS, UQFL36, Box 11F. This willingness of Associations to put up their own candidates is confirmed in a letter from the Marquess of Salisbury to the Second Earl of Selborne, 26 September 1922, George Boyce, ed., *The Crisis of British Unionism: Lord Selborne's Domestic Political Papers, 1885–1922* (London: The Historians Press, 1987), 235–6.

8 Sir George Younger 'Meeting of the Unionist Members of the Cabinet, Wednesday, 26th July 1922', Wilson Papers, Fryer Library, MSS, UQFL36, Box 11F.

9 Lord Alfred Douglas, 'Two Loves', poem.

10 See transcript of the speech at the Carlton Club meeting by Bonar Law, 19 November 1922, PUB207/1, Conservative Party Archive, Bodleian Library. See also 'The Carlton Club Speeches', *The Daily Express*, 20 October 1922, 5.

11 Maynard Colchester Weymss to the King of Siam, 24 October 1922, Gloucester Archives D37/1/444.

12 Forest of Dean 1918 election result: James Wignall (Labour) 9,731 votes; Henry Webb (Liberal, coupon) 5,765 votes. Majority 3,966.

13 Roy Jenkins, *The Chancellors* (London: Papermac, 1999), 206–7.

14 Maynard Colchester Weymss to the King of Siam, 24 October 1922, Gloucester Archives D37/1/444.

15 'Lord Crewe on Liberal Reunion', *The Scotsman*, 24 October 1922, 5.

16 On Conservative Party attitudes towards coalition and its continuance see John Ramsden, *The Age of Balfour and Baldwin, 1902–1940* (London: Longman, 1978), 134–66; David Close, 'Conservatives and Coalition after the First World War', *Journal of Modern History* 45, no. 2 (1973): 240–60; Stanley, 'The Rebel Chief Whip', 224–43.

17 Sir George Younger 'Meeting of the Unionist Members of the Cabinet, Wednesday, 26th July 1922', Wilson Papers, Fryer Library, MSS, UQFL36, Box 11F.

18 'Memorandum of a Conversation with Lord Derby, 8 October 1922', Wilson Papers, Fryer Library, MSS, UQFL36, Box 11F.

19 'Precis of Proceedings at a Meeting at Chamberlain's Dining Room, 11 Downing Street held at 8 p.m. on Tuesday 10th October 1922', Wilson Papers, Fryer Library, MSS, UQFL36, Box 11F.

20 'Election forecast by Sir Malcolm Fraser, 31 December 1921', Austen Chamberlain papers, Cadbury Research Library, AC32/4/1a.

21 'Precis of Proceedings at a Meeting at Chamberlain's Dining Room, 11 Downing Street held at 8 p.m. on Tuesday 10th October 1922', Wilson Papers, Fryer Library, MSS, UQFL36, Box 11F.

22 Sir George Younger to Sir Francis Newdegate (Governor of Western Australia), 17 October 1922, M1539–M1542/Series Bundle 7/File 61, National Library of Australia via Trove, https://nla.gov.au/nla.obj-1484622193/view.

23 Kinnear, *The Fall of Lloyd George*, 60.

24 'Memorandum of Interview with Mr Bonar Law, Wednesday, October 11th, 1922', Wilson Papers, Fryer Library, MSS, UQFL36, Box 11F.

25 'Memorandum of a Short Interview with Mr Chamberlain, 12 October 1922', Wilson Papers, Fryer Library, MSS, UQFL36, Box 11F.

26 Confidential, 16 October 1922, Wilson Papers, Fryer Library, MSS, UQFL36, Box 11F.

27 Confidential, 16 October 1922, Wilson Papers, Fryer Library, MSS, UQFL36, Box 11F.

28 William Bridgeman to his Mother, 13 October 1922, Bridgeman Papers, Shropshire Archives X4629/1/1922/13.

29 William Bridgeman to his Mother, 17 October 1922, Bridgeman Papers, Shropshire Archives, X4629/1/1922/15.

30 'Lord Salisbury's Plain Speech: No More Coalition', *Belfast Telegraph*, 17 October 1922, 7. See also Salisbury to Lord Berwick, 13 October 1922, Conservative and Unionist Association (Ludlow Division), Shropshire Archives, 112/21/5/9/2/1. And telegram to Lord Berwick calling him to the meeting on 13 October 1922, Conservative and Unionist Association (Ludlow Division), Shropshire Archives, X112/21/5/9/2/2.

31 Hugh Cecil to Bill Weigall, Weigall Manuscripts, Kent Archive Service, undated but October-November 1922, U1371/C104/2.

32 Blake, *The Conservative Party from Peel to Churchill*, 206.

33 Samuel Hoare, *Empire of the Air* (London: Collins, 1967), 28–9.

34 'Unionist MP's Decision', *The Times*, 20 October 1922, 8–9.

35 Lynden Livingston Macassey to Sir William Bull, 23 October 1922, Bull Papers 5/6, Churchill College Cambridge.

36 James Younger (the son of Sir George) to Gilmour, 23 October 1922, John Gilmour of Lundin, Fife and Montrave, South Walton, Renfrewshire, GD383/17/20, National Records of Scotland.

37 Gilmour to A. Bartlett Glen, 21 October 1922, Gilmour of Lundin, Fife and Montrave, South Walton, Renfrewshire, GD383/17/18, National Records of Scotland,

38 Election Address by Sir Leslie Scott, Scott Papers, Modern Records Centre, University of Warwick, MSS.119/3/S/LI/13. On the issue of Smith's encouragement to Scott see C. L. Burt (Private Secretary to Lord Birkenhead) to Leslie Scott, 31 October 1922, Scott Papers, Modern Records Centre, University of Warwick, MSS.119/3/S/LI/11.

39 Robert Horne (pencil draft) election address, 25 October 1922, Bull Papers 5/6, Churchill College Cambridge.

40 Bridgeman Papers, Shropshire Archives X4629/a/1/1922/369.

41 'Unionist Party's Future', *The Scotsman*, 23 October 1922, 8.

42 'Lord Derby', *Exeter and Plymouth Gazette*, 23 October 1922, 6. 'No Vendetta', *The Times*, 23 October 1922, 17.

43 'Sir A. Boscawen', *Exeter and Plymouth Gazette*, 23 October 1922, 6.

44 'Kent and the Coalition', *The Times*, 6 November 1922, 14.

45 Chamberlain to G. W. Hubbard, 23 October 1922, Austen Chamberlain papers, Cadbury Research Library, AC33/2/119.

46 'London Letter', *Hull Daily Mail*, 23 October 1922, 4.

47 Lord Beaverbrook, *The Decline and Fall of Lloyd George* (New York: Duell, Sloan and Pearce, 1963), 212.

48 Duncan Watts, *Stanley Baldwin and the Search for Consensus* (London: Hodder and Stoughton, 1996), 24.

49 'Beware the Spellbinders', *Sunday Post*, 22 October 1922, 8.

Chapter 2

The position of the four main parties

The task of defining the electoral relationship between the parties began on 23 October as Bonar Law was appointed leader of the Conservative Party following a meeting at the Hotel Cecil. He then proceeded to Buckingham Palace where King George V asked him to form a government.[1] Chamberlain and the other Tory coalitionists did not attend the meeting at the Hotel Cecil and they would find themselves outside of Bonar Law's new cabinet. Their apparent inaction over previous days was significant given that they did not necessarily have to accept the result of the Carlton Club meeting. Chamberlain, who received a steady stream of letters expressing outrage, consternation and a sense of betrayal over the outcome of the meeting,[2] remained convinced that many Conservatives continued to favour coalition in the interests of national unity, and some of them had urged him to call a meeting of the National Union to argue the case before the wider membership.[3] While he had suspected that he could win the argument, he had concluded that the resulting split in the party would be devastating. Instead, he preferred dignified silence, but the possibility that he might break that silence with potentially devastating consequences for the party was not lost on Bonar Law. The Carlton Club meeting had ended the coalition, but the breach, if handled with anything other than very great care, might yet end the party. As party leader Chamberlain had been mindful of the forces on the right who wanted to be free of Lloyd George. Now Bonar Law as his replacement would have to be very aware of those Conservatives on the centre left who had favoured co-operation over faction, never mind the electoral calculation.

In trying to frame a platform for the new Conservative administration that would not widen the splits in the party, and with which they could go forward to the country in a general election, Bonar Law had the advice of his inner circle. Leo Amery drafted an election address for the new prime minister the day after Bonar Law became party leader. Amery made no secret of the fact that on some issues his intention was for the prime minister to obfuscate, or only to hint at future lines of policy.[4] This was backed by the specific inputs of some of the new ministers as the platform was sharpened.[5] Strikingly, the file in the Bonar Law papers which contains this material also contains historical briefing papers about specific subjects,[6] and copies of speeches by Disraeli, which suggest that Bonar Law, in trying to frame what Conservatism after the First World War meant, was trying to historically ground his vision.[7] That same file also contains notes on what the leading Coalitionist Conservatives were up to during the course of the campaign. The juxtaposition in the same file of papers framing policy, tracing the lines of modern Conservatism, and monitoring the activities of the Conservative Coalitionists is noteworthy. Bonar Law in preparing his platform had a narrow path to tread.

There was also the possibility that some kind of deal might be cut with the Coalition Liberals that would make both electoral sense, and make sense in terms of a divided party. It was with the task of exploring some sort of electoral arrangement with the Coalition Liberals that Sir Malcolm Fraser, principal agent of the Conservative Party, approached Robert Sanders, the deputy party chair.[8] As an under secretary at the War Office Sanders had been one of the generation of young Conservative MPs who had brought down the coalition at the Carlton Club meeting. After the meeting at the Hotel Cecil, Fraser asked Sanders if 'I would see Freddy Guest [former Liberal chief whip and associate of Lloyd George] and try to do a deal as to seats in the country'.[9] In effect Sanders was being asked to be part of a dialogue with the Coalition Liberals to effect a national arrangement, which would be to their mutual interest. Fraser visited Sanders that same evening and Sanders's diary indicates the extent to which things had moved on:

> He came to see me in Eaton Square this evening. He thinks this can be arranged, says L.G. is genuinely afraid of the Labour party, that he is going into the election on the liens of the Leeds speech and that he expects relations to be quite amicable after the election.[10]

The following day Sanders saw Guest and McCurdy. Sanders later commented in his diary: 'Think I have fixed up an arrangement by which we discourage opposition in their seats and they advise their followers to support us' against the Asquithian Liberals.[11] Interestingly, he also commented that Lord Rothermere, the press baron, had been brought into the plot with 'a step in the peerage as his price of his support'.[12] In effect an agreement had been reached which, while not public, and not expressed in detailed form, would see the central parties 'discourage' hostilities and rival campaigns at the local level. The plot was sufficiently well developed to bring in, and buy off, Lord Rothermere to support the pact through his newspapers. That evening Lloyd George on the campaign trail in London warned that 'Unionists alone cannot defend the nation's interests'.[13] Bonar Law reciprocated in a speech in Glasgow on 26 October when he signalled that the door was open to a working relationship with the Lloyd George Liberals. The *Daily Mirror* reported Bonar Law as suggesting: 'There was no reason … why the two parties should not co-operate if each secured fair representation'.[14]

By 26–27 October the two parties appeared to have an understanding to co-operate with each other in the constituencies. However, in a subsequent entry in his diary Sanders went on to say that the deal 'did not come off'.[15] Strikingly, the date of the diary entry is 25 November, some ten days after the day of election. What had happened during the course of the campaign to scupper the deal? Why had the policy of letting local arrangements stand in the interest of mutual understanding between the parties, perhaps formalised into a national arrangement, not been fully realised? What exactly did Sanders mean?

Evidence of the deal could perhaps be found in the behaviour of Freddie Guest as he arrived back in his East Dorset constituency on 26 October. His first meeting was with the local Conservative and Unionist Association rather than his own Liberal supporters. At that meeting, as he recalled the following day to the Executive Committee of his own Liberal Association, Guest gave a pledge of support to a future Bonar Law government if that was the outcome of the election:

> He had informed them that if adopted he intended to stand as a Liberal Anti-Socialist Candidate. They had asked him if he would give to Mr Bonar Law the same loyal co-operation which they had given to Mr Lloyd George, and he had replied that provided Mr Bonar Law avoided reaction on the one hand and revolutionary changes on the other, he saw no reason why he should not co-operate, and that he had instanced cases which he would regard as

> 'reaction', such for example as any attempt to restore the veto of the House of Lords, or to adopt a policy of scuttle with regard to our imperial obligations, which he would resolutely oppose … The result of his meeting with the Unionist Committee had been that they had decided officially to support his Candidature at the impending election presuming he was adopted by his own friends. (Applause.)[16]

The last word, and reaction of the members of the East Dorset Constituency Liberal Association on 27 October as they were told that their prospective Parliamentary Candidate had already been to see the Conservatives is particularly telling.[17] Such was the strength of feeling in favour of continuing to work with the Conservatives that Guest's endorsement as the Liberal Anti-Socialist candidate for East Dorset was carried by over one hundred votes to four in the subsequent meeting of the General Council.[18] The details of Guest's comments to his local association also suggested the potential lines along which a deal might work, whereby Coalition Liberals might give their qualified support to a Bonar Law ministry as the price of continued co-operation.

Throughout the early part of the campaign rumours swirled around Westminster about the possibility of a collaboration between Conservatives and Coalition Liberals at the polls. For example, the *Western Mail* on 24 October, perhaps reflecting the lines of a deal sketched out on the previous day as part of the Fraser-Sanders initiative, hinted at the likely lines of the working relationship between the former coalition partners:

> There may be co-operation between the Conservative and National Liberal parties during and after the general election, but it will not be based upon the Coalition pact of 1918, under which certain lines of policy were laid down, the Premiership was assured to Mr. Lloyd George, and the terms of co-operation in electoral contests strictly defined.[19]

Whatever arrangements might be made for an electoral truce of sorts between the parties at the local level it was very unclear whether good relations would be maintained. Added to the difficulties at the National Level in maintaining the spirit of coalitionism were those within the constituencies. For example, the *Western Mail* also reported on 24 October that in Caerphilly, one of the new seats created in 1918 and held by Labour, plans for Liberals and Conservatives to get behind a single candidate had been jeopardised by the fall of the coalition: 'It is not year clear whether the pact recently made between the Conservatives and Liberals in the Caerphilly Parliamentary Division will hold good ... A few months ago the Conservatives were allowed to select a candidate, the Liberals undertaking to support him as a Coalition candidate'.[20] The appearance of separate parties fighting an election raised question marks over the continuation of such arrangements that the party leaders struggled to contain. In some constituencies local associations were only too ready to end co-operation and to put forward their own candidates. That could threaten the hoped-for co-operation between the parties.

During the last week of October party leaders slowly began to outline the relationships between the parties and the likely direction of politics after the election. Lloyd George, speaking to a meeting of supporters, MPs and candidates at the Hotel Victoria on 25 October, declared that Labour 'has declared relentless war upon us. In self-defence therefore, you have to fight and to resist the onslaughts of the Socialist Party in this country'.[21] He dismissed the Asquithian Liberals because of the hostility of their leader and their willingness to run candidates against some thirty sitting Coalition Liberal seats. Speaking of the Conservatives, Lloyd George was careful to argue:

> If Die-hard candidates are put up either directly or indirectly to attack Coalition-Liberals throughout the country, then we shall have no alternative but to spread the war. If we fall, we will fall fighting, and fighting where we can hit the hardest. And we can do it, but the responsibility will be theirs. We shall certainly not confine our fighting to our own seats.[22]

Of course, to have any sort of effect the threat to 'spread the war' had to be credible both in terms of the capabilities of the Coalition Liberal Organisation and perceptions of those capabilities on the part of the Conservative Party. The latter was perhaps more problematic than the former. In a paper written on 20 October 1921, the general secretary of the Coalition Liberal Party advised that in England and Wales eighty-one seats currently held by Coalition Liberals were considered winnable, with a further thirty-three possible but doubtful.[23] The development of new constituency organisations meant that another twenty-nine seats could be contested with three considered winnable. With the addition of Scottish seats, twenty-five of which had returned Coalition Liberals in

1918, the Coalition Liberal Party were ready to consider contesting around 170 seats. The further expansion of the Coalition Liberal organisation in the constituencies over the next twelve months opened up some further possibilities for seats in which party candidates might be put forward, if not with the hope of winning, then with the realistic possibility that it could spoil the chances of another party. While the general secretary's assessments as to the potential fortunes of the Coalition Liberals at a general election were internal to the party, for Conservative readers the pages of the *Lloyd George Liberal Magazine* contained plenty of indications in the form of 'constituency notes' that the threat to 'spread the war' in October 1922 had to be taken seriously. While it was possible to field a slate of around 170 candidates, the general secretary of the Coalition Liberal Party in a memorandum to the chief whip of 11 September 1922 estimated that thirty-eight seats was the minimum likely return for the Coalition Liberals at the general election.[24] The question was whether to try and consolidate around this caucus and contest a small number of seats, or whether to aim for a larger number that might risk a wider war with the Conservatives that might damage both partys' chances, allowing Labour to claim some unexpected wins. In late October the actions of Conservative diehards in some associations risked this wider war, which both Conservative and Coalition Liberal party hierarchies had no wish to ignite.

It didn't help that during the campaign there was on-going warfare within Coalition Liberal ranks against Charles McCurdy, the chief whip and Scovell the general secretary of the party. An attempt in the midst of the campaign to replace Scovell with Alfred Cope (1877–1954), a career civil servant and fixer for Lloyd George, created confusion and a considerable distraction at Party headquarters.[25] McCurdy objected to the move on the grounds that it would be madness to get rid of Scovell at this point, and might derail the campaign. Scovell, in consequence, would stay on until after the poll with Cope as his shadow and eventual replacement.[26] As a backdrop to fighting an election the tensions between Scovell and Cope were less than ideal.

Notes

1 'Mr Bonar Law Takes Office as Prime Minister', *Daily Mirror*, 24 October 1923, 3.

2 For examples see Austen Chamberlain papers, Cadbury Research Library, AC33/2/96-119.

3 See Chamberlain's remarks on a dinner given in his honour by his friends, 30 November 1922, Austen Chamberlain papers, Cadbury Research Library, AC33/2/148.

4 Leo Amery to Bonar Law, 24 October 1922, Bonar Law papers BL110/1/1.

5 See Anderson Montagu-Barlow (Minister of Labour) to Bonar Law, 25 October 1922, Bonar Law papers BL110/1/1. 1st Earl Peel (Secretary of State for India) to Bonar Law, 24 October 1922, Bonar Law papers BL110/1/1.

6 See for example, Agriculture in England, 1895–1914 (undated and anonymous), Bonar Law papers BL110/1/2.

7 See for example, 'The Spirit of the Landed Interest, Disraeli (1849)', and 'Extract of a Speech Delivered by Mr Disraeli at Manchester (1872)', Bonar Law papers BL110/1/2.

8 Robert Sanders, 1st Baron Bayford, (1867–1940), Conservative and Coalition Conservative MP for Bridgwater (1910–23), Government Deputy Chief Whip (1918–19), Junior Lord of the Treasury (1919–21), Under-Secretary of State at the War Office (1921–22), Minister of Agriculture and Fisheries (1922–24).

9 Sanders diary entry, 23 October 1922, John Ramsden, ed., *Real Old Tory Politics: The Political Diaries of Robert Sanders, Lord Bayford 1910–1935* (London: The Historians Press, 1984), 192.

10 Sanders diary entry, 23 October 1922, Ramsden, *Real Old Tory Politics*, 192.

11 Sanders diary entry, 25 October 1922, Ramsden, *Real Old Tory Politics*, 192.

12 Sanders diary entry, 25 October 1922, Ramsden, *Real Old Tory Politics*, 192.

13 'Mr Lloyd George's Cry of Britain First', *Daily Mirror*, 26 October 1922, 3.

14 'Mr Bonar Law Announces a "Negative" Policy', *Daily Mirror*, 27 October 1922, 3.

15 Sanders diary entry, 25 November 1922, Ramsden, *Real Old Tory Politics*, 193.

16 Special Meeting of the Executive Committee, 27 October 1922, East Dorset Liberal Association, Dorset History Centre, D.1512.1

17 Special Meeting of the Executive Committee, 27 October 1922, East Dorset Liberal Association, Dorset History Centre, D.1512.1

18 Special Meeting of the General Council, 30 October 1922, East Dorset Liberal Association, Dorset History Centre, D.1512.1.

19 'The New Leader', *Western Mail*, 24 October 1922, 6.

20 'Caerphilly', *Western Mail*, 24 October 1922, 6.

21 'Lloyd George's Policy', *Westminster Gazette*, 26 October 1922, 8.

22 'Lloyd George's Policy', *Westminster Gazette*, 26 October 1922, 8.

23 'Election Forecast', 20 October 1921, Scovell Papers, Lloyd George Archive.

24 'Scovell Memorandum to the Chief Whip [presented Prior to his Meeting with the Prime Minister 11 September 1922] – Election Prospects by Seat, 11 September 1922', Scovell Papers, Lloyd George Archive.

25 On Cope see for example, Thomas Jones, Diary 24 June 1921, 13–17 August 1921; 30 October 1921; 12 November 1921 in Keith Middlemas, ed., *Thomas Jones: Whitehall Diary*, vol. 3 (London: Oxford University Press, 1971), 79–81, 98–101, 150–51, 162–3. Thomas Jones Diary, 23 October 1922, in Middlemas, ed., *Thomas Jones: Whitehall Diary*, vol. 1 (London: Oxford University Press, 1969), 217.

26 Scovell to J.T. Davies, 30 October 1922, enclosed in Scovell to McCurdy, 30 October 1922, Scovell Papers, Lloyd George Archive. See also McCurdy to Scovell, 30 October 1922, Scovell Papers, Lloyd George Archive.

Chapter 3

Locally arranged pacts

As the leaders attempted to define the relationship between the parties, both Conservative and Coalition Liberal candidates did what they could within their constituencies to maintain cross-party support. In Dundee, Churchill, handicapped by illness, and facing a particularly strong challenge from the socialists, issued an appeal that stressed that he would conduct his campaign so as to convince Conservatives that electing two Liberals for the city was in the best interests of the British Empire and stability at home.[1] Some coalition-minded Conservatives, imperilled by the same leftward drift of parts of the electorate, issued similar appeals. For example, in Glasgow Hillhead the Unionist MP Sir Robert Horne, chancellor of the exchequer from 1921 until the fall of the coalition, faced challenges from Labour and the Asquithian Liberals.[2] As one of the Chamberlain loyalists who had refused to accept Bonar Law's offer of ministerial office, his was a potentially lonely fight and he made a public appeal to both Unionists and Liberals who believed in both party principle and co-operation as being in the national interest. Likewise, in the two-member Norwich constituency the Lloyd George Liberal Edward Hilton Young was willing to give a public promise of 'qualified support' to Bonar Law's government as the price of persuading local Unionists not to run candidates against himself and George Robertson.[3] At Ilkeston, Marshall Freeman, the Conservative candidate who had stood aside in 1918, to give General John Seely[4] (armed with the coupon), a free run at the seat for the Coalition Liberals, wrote a letter to one of his supporters that was published in the local press:

> If General Seeley is prepared to give assurances of support to Mr. Bonar Law, and the Prime Minister is content to accept the

> same, my appearance as an Independent Conservative candidate might have unfortunate results. On the other hand, having regard to General Seely's expressed views on the Safeguarding of Industries Act and other topics, I imagine it may be somewhat difficult for him to promise unreserved support for the new ministry.[5]

In fact, by 1922 the policy positions of Seeley (a former Conservative MP) appeared increasingly difficult to define with any precision so that both Conservatives, Coalition Liberals and Asquithian Liberals had hopes for the veteran politician.

In London, also, the possibility of local party pacts was underpinned by the willingness of some Coalition Liberals to give promises of support to a future Conservative government under Bonar Law. As Chris Cook has noted: 'In London, Macnamara in Camberwell North-West, as well as Arthur Lever in Hackney Central and Lt.-Col. M. Alexander in Southwark South East, received official Conservative support only after they had given specific pledges of support to a Bonar Law Ministry'.[6] In Southwark South East the need for co-operation was especially pointed. In 1921 the seat had been captured by Labour candidate Thomas Naylor[7] with a majority of 3,925 votes, but on a turnout of just 38.5 per cent and with the intervention of an Independent Conservative candidate. The Labour victory in 1921 had underlined the need for the parties to work together if they were to avoid the same eventuality at the 1922 General Election.

There were similar examples beyond London of Coalition Liberals being willing to give full or partial pledges of support to a potential future Bonar Law government. For example, there was a strong desire for continuing party co-operation underpinned by a pledge in the Forest of Dean which had been captured by Labour in 1918 with a majority of 3,966. Such was the strength of the Labour majority that in 1922 the Conservative Association was willing to continue standing aside after Winnifred Combe Tennant, the Coalition Liberal candidate, offered a limited pledge to 'give a general support to Bonar Law [if after the election he was able to form a government] in all questions of today affecting Foreign Affairs'.[8] The identification of foreign affairs as the principal focus of a pledge to Bonar Law seems to have been a reflection of local concerns that it was on matters of foreign policy where Lloyd George had so badly strayed from good sense, and the established practices of British government, and where co-operation 'in the national interest' was so urgently required. With a well-entrenched Labour candidate the local Association undoubtedly concluded that without a united anti-socialist vote the seat would again fall to Labour.

Continuing calls for Liberal-Conservative co-operation also came from some of those in the safest of Conservative seats. Sir Laming Worthington-Evans, the member for Colchester and former Secretary of State for War, who had declined to continue as a minister under Bonar Law, made a particularly forthright appeal for continued coalition on 26 October focussing press attention on his constituency and generating some controversy within it.[9] In defence of the case for Conservative coalitionism he described himself as 'a Tory, [who] has always been a Tory, and will remain a Tory to the end'.[10] Strikingly, he drew a distinction between the terms Conservative and Tory, the latter of which he defined as 'fixed, unbending invincible adherence to old, traditional, party principles'. *The Times* correspondent commented, in a display of that paper's attitudes towards the split in Conservative ranks that Worthington-Evans in his speech came over as less Tory and more 'Liberal-Conservative' in his continued support for Lloyd George as 'the greatest man in Europe'.[11] In a campaign in which many of the most ardent 'Liberal-Conservatives' were hedging their bets, or keeping their thoughts about the outcome of the election largely silent, the speech by Worthington-Evans was noteworthy for its passion, its prediction of continued coalition, and the tracing of division within the Conservative Party.

The Duke of Sutherland's speech the following day, 27 October, at Carshalton in Mitcham, Surrey, was more typical in its gentle calls for co-operation, coupled with suggestions to all 'Unionists and Conservatives to rally to the standard of Mr Bonar Law'.[12] In effect the calls for co-operation (and in effect for Liberals to back the Conservative candidate if Labour put forward a candidate in the constituency) found common cause with the politics of the speech being given by a Scottish Conservative. Evidence of the acceptability to the party hierarchy of calls for continued co-operation between Conservatives and Liberals was evidenced just four days later when the duke was appointed Under-Secretary of State for Air.

In practice, during the last week of October, it was apparent to both the leadership of the Conservative Party, to hopeful candidates, and others that a certain constructive ambiguity around the issue of coalition at the party level had its advantages. In areas where socialists were a threat to sitting Conservatives the idea of continued co-operation might head off the emergence of a Labour candidate. For example, following the Duke of Sutherland's speech, no Labour candidate was forthcoming at Mitcham, and the sitting Conservative candidate would be returned. Robert Horne in Glasgow Hillhead similarly avoided a socialist challenge in 1922. Elsewhere, Conservative candidates challenged by Labour hopefuls could hope to secure some measure of Liberal support amidst the calls for continued co-operation. Bonar Law himself, at Glasgow Central, was to be one of the principal beneficiaries of this, as the pendulum began to swing against him. In Conservative stronghold seats expressing anti-coalition sentiment, and a detestation of the mercurial Lloyd George, this could serve to rally the Conservative faithful grown weary of coalition and a problematic prime minister. The election of 1922 really was a case of 'horses for courses' and their political jockeys could select their riding colours from a veritable palette of Tory blue and Coalition Liberal yellow blurring into each other to the point of a utilitarian camouflage political green. The attitude of the Conservative Party, and the Coalition Liberal Party in not defining their relationship too closely, was essential in this process. In 1922 the first rule of coalition was not to talk too openly about coalition except in seats where the threat of Labour was particularly marked. Yet, across the country, and largely irrespective of local circumstance, evidence could be found of the willingness of Conservative candidates to extend the hand to former coalition colleagues. Even in true blue Chelsea, Samuel Hoare, one of the prime movers behind the Carlton Club meeting, facing a solitary candidate in the form of Bertrand Russell (Labour), at least put in his election address a suggestion that the Conservatives were 'ready to co-operate with all those who agree with us'.[13]

If working relationships were being negotiated between Conservatives and Coalition Liberals at the constituency and national levels then a similar process was taking place between Liberals of both hues in some of the metropolitan areas. While relationships between the party leaderships were simply too strained to permit immediate re-unification at the national level, at the local level some groups of Liberals were prepared to bury their differences in the interests of 'Free Trade' and unity against common enemies. In Manchester, a traditional bastion of Free Trade Liberalism, and Leeds (on the other side of the Pennines), together with Southampton, Liberal re-unification was substantially achieved before polling day. Liberals would not stand against Liberals and Liberal candidates would stand without particular affiliation to either Asquith or Lloyd George. In Leeds, for example, with two of the six constituencies held by Labour (Leeds North East and South East) it seemed likely that any division in Liberal ranks would lead to Labour breakthroughs. In Leeds South, Central and West the Coalition Liberal Candidate would contest the seats they had won as Lloyd George Liberals in 1918. Only in Leeds North did the candidate from 1918 not fight the seat in 1922, and that seems to have been down to his desire to stand down. Strikingly Lloyd George gave the appearance of having only limited knowledge about these Liberal reunions. In a speech on 4 November in which he took the platform with Austen Chamberlain and Sir Arthur Griffith Boscawen, he noted 'there are pacts also, I believe between the two wings of the Liberal Party in some of the towns in the North – (A VOICE – "Manchester" – and Leeds, I believe)'.[14] The extent to which different political parties were reaching out to each other was noteworthy but perhaps Lloyd George had no strong desire to focus attention on the deals that were emerging during the campaign.

Notes

1 Churchill to Robertson (President, Dundee Liberal Association to be read out to electors), 27 October 1922, Churchill Papers CHAR5/28A/20–30.

2 Robert Horne (1871–1940), Unionist MP Glasgow Hillhead (1918–1937), Minister of Labour (1919–20), President of the Board of Trade (1920–21), Chancellor of the Exchequer (1921–22).

3 'Facing Both Ways', *Westminster Gazette*, 26 October 1922, 8. Edward Hilton Young (1879–1960), Coalition Liberal MP Norwich (1915–22), Liberal MP for Norwich (1924–26), Conservative MP for Norwich (1926–29), Conservative MP for Sevenoaks (1929–35), Minister of Health (1931–35). George Roberts (1868–1928), Labour MP for Norwich (1906–1918), Coalition Labour MP for Norwich (1918–22), Coalition Liberal MP for Norwich (1922–23), Parliamentary Secretary to the Board of Trade (1916–17), Minister of Labour (1917–19), Minister of Food Control (1919–20).

4 John Edward Bernard Seely, 1st Baron Mottistone (1868–1947), Conservative MP for Isle of Wight (1900–06), Liberal MP for Liverpool Abercromby (1906–10), Liberal and then Coalition Liberal MP for Ilkeston (1910–22), Under-Secretary of State for the Colonies (1908–10), Under-Secretary of State for War (1911–12), Secretary of State for War (1912–14).

5 'Gen. Seeley Challenged', *Nottingham Journal*, 26 October 1922, 5.

6 Cook, *The Age of Alignment*, 17. Arthur Lever (1860–1924), Liberal MP for Harwich (1906–1910), Coalition Liberal MP for Hackney Central (1922–23). Maurice Alexander (1889–1945), Coalition Liberal MP for Southwark South East (1922–23).

7 Thomas Naylor (1868–1958), Labour MP for Southwark South East (1921–22, 1923–31, 1935–50).

8 Maynard Colchester Weymss to the King of Siam, 11 November 1922, Gloucester Archives D37/1/446.

9 See 'Election correspondence', Laming Worthington-Evans Papers, MS.Eng. hist. c.892., Bodleian Library.

10 'True Blue Tories for Essex', *The Times*, 27 October 1922, 14.

11 'True Blue Tories for Essex', *The Times*, 27 October 1922, 14.

12 'The Duke of Sutherland on the Coalition', *The Times*, 28 October 1922, 12.

13 'To the Parliamentary Electors for the Borough of Chelsea', 1 November 1922, GBR/0012/MS, Templewood/S/Scrapbook 12/7, Templewood Papers, Cambridge University Library.

14 'Ex-Premier on the Pacts', *The Times*, 6 November 1922, 10.

Chapter 4

'There is no Pact – But'

If politically it was difficult for the party leaders in the aftermath of the Carlton Club meeting to discuss the possibility of a future coalition, or the strategic logic of a pact between the Conservative and Lloyd George Liberals, then it did not prevent the parties at the local level from making their own arrangements. In areas such as Scotland and Lancashire these were overt, to the exasperation of some in the Conservative ranks. In the early days of the election the special correspondent of *The Times* reporting on the visit of Bonar Law to Scotland expressed his exasperation: 'Definite arrangements have been made in regard to practically every constituency that there be no rivalry. Such a policy means nothing more nor less than coalition at the election as well as co-operation afterwards'.[1] As the *Western Daily Press* declared on 30 October: 'There is no Pact – But'.[2] The *Daily Mirror* was less coy, running the headline: 'The "Don't-Know-Where-We-Are" Election Maze: Nation Bewildered by Sharing of Seats by Parties Who Deny "Coupon Pact"'.[3] Meanwhile, the *Daily Mail* on 30 October carried a cartoon of a grave with the caption 'Coalition's Body Lies a Mouldering in the Grave – But its Soul Goes Marching On', complete with a figure marching out of the grave in the direction of a signpost pointing to 'The Constituencies'.[4]

The rumours that a secret pact at the national level was in existence were so extensive that Sir George Younger had to issue a statement that 'No Pact of any kind exists'.[5] What was noticed on many sides, though, and what mystified many Coalition Liberal activists, was the former prime minister's complete lack of enthusiasm for attacking the Conservatives and responding to local challenges to sitting Coalition Liberals. As *The Times* noted: 'A good many National Liberals are astonished at the meekness with which Mr Lloyd George has suffered these assaults on seats that National Liberals have held'.[6] To many observers the evidence for the existence of a pact seemed obvious.

This was further underpinned throughout the campaign by press reports that supported the idea that ordinary voters had much to fear from the revolutionary socialism of the Labour Party, its union backers, and from the Communist International which exercised influence over the left in Britain. The *Sheffield Daily Telegraph* on the day before polling was particularly blunt with a report headed 'Lenin watching Britain – "Soviet's" Hopes based on Labour's Chances – "Reds" Come out into the Open'.[7] The report was supported on the same page by an account of how Winston Churchill had been shouted down by 'Reds' at Dundee and an appeal to women voters to 'Crush the menace' of Socialism.[8]

As Laura Beers has demonstrated in her work on electoral betting in inter-war Britain, investors in October-November 1922 were concerned at the likelihood of a hung Parliament, and a further election in 1923 which might deliver a Labour government: 'In the run-up to the November 1922 election … insurers were selling policies to indemnify investors not only against the possibility of a Labour victory … but against the possibility of a second general election returning a Labour government before February 1923'.[9] The Red Scare of 1922 was a reminder of the socialist threat in particular constituencies, and the overall emergence of Labour as a potential party of government. 'Co-operation' to forestall the progress of socialism made obvious sense.

Many Conservatives and Asquithians were appalled at what they saw as the attempt to secure coalition by the back door. On 27 October Asquith launched into an attack:

> Mr Asquith in the course of his address to an enthusiastic audience at Peterborough yesterday advanced the contention that the 'co-operation' of which so much is heard nowadays is only another equivalent for the out of fashion term 'Coalition' … It must be admitted that the future relationship of the Conservatives under Mr. Bonar Law and the National Liberals led by Mr Lloyd George is not easy to state with any certainty, and the position in certain constituencies where local arrangements have been arrived at is still more puzzling. Yesterday from London came a report that 'the suggestion that a compact has been entered into between Unionists and Coalition

> Liberals was emphatically denied to-day at the Conservative headquarters.' Mr Law's speech at Glasgow contained a passage much to the same effect. According to this the new firm has no connection with the old, although some of the partners in the original combination have crossed over to take seats on the reconstructed board of directors.[10]

While most Asquithians could do little but cry foul, there were those within Conservative ranks prepared to take a more direct approach. The question was whether their intervention could spark a wider reaction within the Conservative Party against the party truce.

The evolution of Conservative Party policy after the Carlton Club meeting, and the unofficial truce with the Coalition Liberals, was much to the distaste of Lord Beaverbrook, the pro-tariff newspaper baron and long-time friend of Bonar Law. Beaverbrook had been pivotal to the breakaway of the Conservatives from the coalition as Samuel Hoare noted: 'Throughout the October crisis Beaverbrook's was the advice that chiefly counted with his friend. It was confident when Bonar Law was doubting, and concrete and practical when Bonar Law was brooding moodily over the fire in a state of ... inaction'.[11] Beaverbrook's flagship *Daily Express* had publicly encouraged the party to break away from the coalition and was thunderous in its endorsement of Conservatism. It promised its readers on 23 October:

> (1.) A Conservative Government would mean the end of a policy of foreign adventure, which has cost us millions, brought us nothing, and nearly plunged us into a wanton war. The Government would stand pledged to clear out of Constantinople, Mesopotamia, and Palestine.
>
> (2.) This would leave Conservatism free to obey its natural instincts and look after its own people first. It would develop our home industries and imperial markets, and so decrease unemployment and launch us on the path of returning prosperity.
>
> (3.) Mr Bonar Law can be trusted to pursue a safe and saving course at home as well as abroad. There would be an end of those ambitious schemes which cost millions, tax industry, depress credit and end in a financial fiasco.
>
> (4.) Conservatism stands for the liberty and harmless enjoyment of the subject. It does not love kill-joys or restrictive laws.[12]

With Bonar Law at the helm Beaverbrook was certain that the new government would deliver on the policies advocated by the *Express*. However, Beaverbrook felt deeply let down when Bonar Law informed him, shortly after the general election campaign had begun, that the group of senior Conservatives (including Curzon and Derby) called together to frame policy for the election had advised against campaigning on a platform of tariff reform. Beaverbrook was aghast. He later described it as a 'disaster'.[13] That Bonar Law informed Beaverbrook that it was the decision of this inner group speaks volumes about how the new prime minister regarded the likely reaction of the newspaperman to policy for the forthcoming election. This did not prevent Beaverbrook from writing an extensive piece for *The Daily Mirror*, in a 'Grand Bonar Law Number', in which the newspaperman gave fulsome praise to the Conservative leader. Bonar Law was described as the 'Most Likeable of Men' and 'Something Different' and someone on whom the electorate could rely.[14] Whatever their private differences, in public the relationship was presented as being most harmonious.

As the campaign took shape, and it appeared that party pacts would be maintained in many areas Beaverbrook grew increasingly angry at what he perceived as the willingness of the Conservative leadership to accept that the likely outcome of the election would be coalition in some new form. As he later wrote in *The Decline and Fall of Lloyd George* published in the 1960s: 'It was a case of the old Coalition all over again under a new name … The old bad policies would be continued. The sins of Mr. Lloyd George and his colleagues would be visited on Bonar Law and the new Administration'.[15] In Beaverbrook's thinking the Labour Party and Asquithian Liberals would very quickly be able to re-ignite feelings against the coalition with the Conservative Party catching most of the blame for the new/old arrangement. As a result, he set out to destabilise the relationship between the former coalition partners. Informing Sir George Younger, Beaverbrook sought to put forward candidates against sitting National Liberals and in others he paid the election expenses of candidates where constituency associations were ready to put forward their own nominees. In *The Decline and Fall of Lloyd George* Beaverbrook details his actions without identifying the constituencies where he attempted to intervene.[16] Beaverbrook was a man much given to maximising his own importance.

A comparison between the initial survey of expected nominees carried out by *The Times* on 27 October, and those appearing on the ballot paper in

1922 does suggest that only a small number of Independent Conservatives came forward to contest the 1922 election (a maximum of twenty), and the majority of these were clearly not Beaverbrook candidates (a likely maximum of three).[17] For example, in Westminster St George's the seat was eventually won by the sitting MP James Erskine as an Independent Conservative. He had initially been elected in a 1921 by-election as an Anti-Waste candidate but by 1922 the Anti-Waste campaign was all but over and a fresh label was required. The labels independent Unionist and Conservative and Anti-Waste were used interchangeably to describe Erskine's candidature. Beaverbrook's desire for 'scuttle' in the Middle East meant there was some policy alignment between his goals and the policy favoured by the Anti-Waste movement, but there is no evidence that Erskine's campaign was under-written by the Canadian newspaper baron.[18] If Beaverbrook did put money into a larger number of candidates then he wasted his money. Only three Independent Conservatives would be elected, and only in East Dorset can we see clear evidence of Beaverbrook's hand.

This is not to rule out the possibility that Beaverbrook's actions did not serve as encouragement to a number of Conservative Associations to bring forth their own 'official' candidates that then received Central Office backing. Some of these may initially have been Independent Conservative candidates subsequently adopted by the Association. The sources do not allow the figures to be established with any certainty but what we can see is that between 27 October and 6 November a small but potentially significant number of Conservative nominees were added to the poll that caused some panic in Coalition Liberal ranks. Across Scotland the truce between the parties held good with just two interventions across seventy seats. In the fifty-nine London seats only in Bermondsey West and Bethnal Green North East did two Conservatives (one of whom was an Independent Conservative) come forward between the two dates to raise the prospect of a wider assault against the Coalition Liberals. Likewise in the English Counties only around ten Conservatives (official and independent) came forward to be added to the ballot paper between 27 October and 6 November and some of this was no doubt local associations taking their time with the process. In Wales, however, something more significant was taking place. In five of the twety-four Welsh seats Unionist candidates were nominated in the lead up to the close of nominations. Those five seats (Camarthen, Denbigh, Wrexham, Flintshire and Aberavon were considered likely to return Coalition Liberal Candidates and, in the event, the intervention of Unionists would cause two of those seats to fall to Labour including Aberavon to future Labour Prime Minister Ramsay MacDonald. This late Unionist assault on the bastion of Lloyd George Liberalism suggested both co-ordination and a sign that the party truce might break down altogether with local associations, given moral encouragement from Beaverbrook, preparing to set aside existing agreements and fielding their own candidates. In some panic senior Coalition Liberals considered how to hit back at Beaverbrook and to re-inforce the party truce with Conservative Central Office. For example, on 31 October Sir Alfred Mond, speaking at Swansea, said that the British public needed to know whether it was 'Lord Beaverbrook's Government or Mr. Bonar Law's. If Lord Beaverbrook wished to rule the country, he at least should have the courage to take the responsibility of office'.[19]

The late emergence of Conservative candidates also rankled with some Conservatives who could see the likelihood that Labour was going to be gifted seats. For example, in the Forest of Dean Constituency in Gloucestershire Augustus Dinnick (Independent Conservative) threw his hat into the campaign in apparent challenge of the local Conservative Association's decision to back the Coalition Liberal candidate, Winifred Coombe Tennant, after she had given a pledge to support a future Bonar Law government in the conduct of foreign affairs.[20] One senior member of the Association expressed his anger at the interjection: 'At the last moment a stranger, a regular "carpet-bagger" came forward as a Conservative quite unsupported by the Local Association or the Heads of the Party in London'.[21] Such potential interventions raised the temperature within both parties as the closing date for nominations approached.

Concern at the potential impact of Beaverbrook's action by leading Coalition Liberals led leading Coalition Liberals to approach him to see if he would break off his campaign. This involved a meeting between the newspaper magnate, Freddie Guest and Lord Birkenhead (one of the Conservative Coalitionists overthrown at the Carlton Club meeting). The meeting ended in acrimony as Beaverbrook refused to give National Liberals an easy ride. As Beaverbrook explains in *The Decline and Fall of Lloyd George*: 'There was nothing doing. Tory candidates would be launched against the lot. "What! Against Churchill too?" Yes, against Churchill too. The visitors became angry. How could I go against my old and trusted friends'.[22]

In Guest's case the personal rupture was considerable. In January 1918 Guest had played a significant role in getting Beaverbrook appointed as Minister for Propaganda.[23] He wrote to Beaverbrook in distinctly hurt tones to remind the newspaperman of how he had helped him to get into government, and had defended him from accusations that he was nothing more than an adventurer with little scruple and overweening ambition.[24]

On 5 November, Beaverbrook dismissed Guest's letter in contemptuous fashion:

> I have no desire to disturb the friendship to which you refer. I therefore overlook your observation about 'tricky politics' ... I also appreciate the personal defence you have made of me against charges, which never had behind them the slightest foundation in fact. But I will remind you that we have both lived in a stormy atmosphere, and that I have often pleaded your cause in our own society ... I really do not feel inclined to go into a kind of balance sheet of the past services we may have done each other in politics – except to deny the suggestion that I desired office, or accepted it at your hands ... I pass on to the issue of public policy which is, after all, really the thing that matters. Your proposal appears to be that I should withdraw opposition on account of friendship. This argument did not move me when Churchill insisted on fighting the Russians, and it does not move me now when you and your friends are turned out for trying to fight the Turks ... I cannot put you in a category apart in response to an appeal based on friendship. As to East Dorset I am not responsible for Hall Caine though I will support him.[25]

The intervention of Beaverbrook was an unwelcome development for both Coalition Liberals and co-operation-minded Conservatives but its significance at the constituency level is impossible to quantify, given the probably covert interactions between the newspaper baron and local associations.

Notes

1 'The General Election', *The Times*, 25 October 1922, 8.

2 'There is no Pact – But', *Western Daily Press*, 30 October 1922, 10.

3 *The Daily Mirror*, 30 October 1922, 3.

4 *The Daily Mail*, 30 October 1922, 6.

5 'There is no Pact – But', *Western Daily Press*, 30 October 1922, 10.

6 'Strength of Parties – Nearly 1,400 Candidates – Ex-Premier's Hidden Army', *The Times*, 4 November 1922, 10.

7 'Lenin Watching Britain', *Sheffield Daily Telegraph*, 14 November 1922, 7.

8 'Howled Down' and 'The Communists', *Sheffield Daily Telegraph*, 14 November 1922, 7.

9 Laura D. Beers, 'Punting on the Thames: Electoral Betting in Interwar Britain', *Journal of Contemporary History* 45, no. 2 (2010): 282–314 (289).

10 'Co-operation or Coalition?', *Western Daily Press*, 28 October 1922, 12.

11 Hoare, *Empire of the Air*, 34.

12 'Policy of the Daily Express', *The Daily Express*, 23 October 1922, 1.

13 Beaverbrook, *The Decline and Fall of Lloyd George*, 212.

14 'Andrew Bonar Law – the Man', *The Daily Mirror*, 8 November 1922, 6.

15 Beaverbrook, *The Decline and Fall of Lloyd George*, 213.

16 Beaverbrook, *The Decline and Fall of Lloyd George*, 214.

17 'The General Election: The Times List of Candidates', *The Times*, 27 October 1922, 8. 'The Nominations', *The Times*, 6 November 1922, 20.

18 'Palestine and Mesopotamia: Election Issues in London', *The Daily Mail*, 1 November 1922, 6.

19 'The Red's aims', *Sheffield Daily Telegraph*, 1 November 1922, 10.

20 For Winifred Coombe Tennant Papers relating to the election see Coombe Tennant papers, South Glamorgan Archives Service, GB 216 DD T/7/11/1/hub.

21 Maynard Colchester Weymss to the King of Siam, 11 November 1922, Gloucester Archives D37/1/446.

22 Beaverbrook, *The Decline and Fall of Lloyd George*, 215.

23 Guest to Lloyd George, 23 January 1918, Lloyd George Papers LG/F/21/2/11.

24 Guest to Beaverbrook, 3 November 1922, Beaverbrook to Guest, 5 November 1922, BBK/G/12–13, 1st Baron Beaverbrook, Parliamentary Archives.

25 Guest to Beaverbrook, 3 November 1922, Beaverbrook to Guest, 5 November 1922, BBK/G/12–13, 1st Baron Beaverbrook, Parliamentary Archives.

Chapter 5

'Co-operation' in the constituencies

The rising panic within the Coalition Liberal camp, partly as a result of Beaverbrook's self-publicised shenanigans, did not prevent the maintenance of good harmony between the parties across most of the country at the local level. As Chris Wrigley has argued in his overview chapter on the history of Conservative-Liberal coalitions in British politics: 'the Conservative Party's rank and file and many MPs have not liked coalitions. They have suffered them in the hope that they serve to thwart Labour ... or as staging posts between opposition and majority Conservative administrations'.[1] In 1922 both issues were at stake and, even beyond the ranks of Scottish and Lancashire Conservatives, there were party members who remained convinced of the need for continued co-operation, and Coalition Liberals prepared to meet them half-way.

For example, Coalition Liberal MP Hilton Young in Norwich appealed to Conservatives to back him against the Labour Party who he described as 'The real enemy'.[2] He, and George Roberts (patriotic Labour) also faced a possible challenge from Asquithian Liberals. Similarly, in East Leicester there was a keen desire between Conservatives and Coalition Liberals to work together. The seat had been won for the Coalition Liberals in 1918, but at the by-election in 1922 caused by Sir Gordon Hewart's[3] entry into the House of Lords as Lord Chief Justice, the seat had fallen to the Labour candidate, partly because of the intervention of Ronald Allen[4] for the Asquithian Liberals. There was an eagerness to ensure that Labour did not retain the seat at the general election. The desire for co-operation at Leicester East was noted in the national press:

> Cooperation is a real thing in Leicester. Since the last election there has been an excellent relationship between the local Unionists and

> the Liberal followers to Mr. Lloyd George, and regret is expressed that it has been found necessary for the leaders to part company. The rank and file, however, show no disposition to embark on what they regard as a fratricidal conflict, and there is evidence of understanding, if not of actual formal compact.[5]

The desire to keep Labour out of Leicester East was seemingly shared by the Asquith Liberals, as Ronald Allen was persuaded that Leicester South and a straight fight against the Conservative candidate, might be a better bet.

The same desire for co-operation could be found in many other constituencies where Liberalism and Conservatism faced a strong challenge from the Labour Party. At Camborne in 1918, as a seat in which no coupon was issued, the Asquithian Liberal Francis Acland had beaten the Labour candidate by just 532 votes. Following the election, the Lloyd George Liberals and Conservatives of the constituency had come together to express their desire to secure for the next election a joint candidate more wholeheartedly in support of the principle of continued coalition under Lloyd George.[6] As Acland made plans to stand for the Tiverton constituency the Lloyd George Liberals and Conservatives made plans to search for a new candidate. With the hard rock mining industry in and around Camborne and Redruth going through considerable difficulties, there was a good chance that Labour could break through at the polls. The selection of Sir William Beddoe Rees, Welsh non-conformist and architect, satisfied both camps, especially as he agreed to financially support both the Liberal and Conservative Associations.[7] As the election got underway in the constituency, Sir John Green was careful to signal to local Conservatives that 'local arrangements' would continue in a seat where the Conservatives seemingly had no chance:

> I daresay it is likely that what was known as the Coalition Liberal candidate will remain the candidate of the Camborne Division … If so, I have no doubt that the Unionists of the division will loyally abide by their past decision to give him their support … I hardly think the two forces will run separately in this division seeing that you have two other candidates – Mr. Leif Jones [Asquithian Liberal], who wants us all to drink tea, and the Labour candidate, who wants to nationalise almost everything.[8]

The one difficulty was that Beddoe Rees had already agreed to 'jump ship' and stand in Bristol South which was closer to his home and business interests in South Wales. Fortunately, an even better candidate had been found for the mining seat in the form of Captain Algernon Moreing, previously MP for Buckrose in Yorkshire, who was named as Coalition Liberal candidate for the division on 26 October.[9] As a mining engineer with a distinguished war record, Moreing came across as a very credible candidate who could understand and represent the difficulties facing the mine owners and the miners. His pockets were deep enough to ensure financial support for both constituency associations.[10]

In some seats where the Conservatives were considered to have a good chance of taking the seat the sense of fair play and personal loyalties of the local party leadership limited the challenges facing sitting Coalition Liberal MPs. For example, in East Dorset where Freddie Guest faced the challenge of an unofficial 'Conservative' candidate secured by Beaverbrook, the local Conservative Association refused to endorse the press baron's man. Guest had hinted strongly that he would support a future Bonar Law government if that was the outcome of the election, and the window of his party office in Poole displayed portraits of both Lloyd George and Bonar Law.[11] To many members of the local association it made no sense to split the anti-socialist revolt by endorsing a carpet-bagger outsider. Their resolve was underlined by a letter from Sir George Younger to the effect that without the support of the local association Beaverbrook's candidate would receive no official party endorsement at either local or national level.[12]

Notes

1 Chris Wrigley, 'Coalition Blues: The Conservatives, the Liberals and Conservative-Liberal Coalitions in Britain since 1895', in *The Foundations of the British Conservative Party: Essays on Conservatism from Lord Salisbury to David Cameron*, ed. Bradley W. Hart and Richard Carr (London: Bloomsbury, 2013), 174.

2 'Cross-Currents in Norwich', *The Times*, 25 October 1922, 8.

3 Gordon Hewart, 1st Viscount Hewart (1870–1943), Liberal MP for Leicester 1913–18 and Coalition Liberal MP for East Leicester (1918–22), Solicitor General (1916–19), Attorney General (1919–22), Lord Chief Justice (1922–40).

4 Ronald Allen (1889–1936), Liberal MP for South Leicester (1923–24).

5 'Cooperation at Leicester', *The Times*, 2 November 1922, 14.

6 For Acland's relationship with local Conservatives see minutes 1919–22 of the Conservative and Unionist Association (Cambourne Division), Kresen Kernow, X387.

7 Sir William Beddoe Rees (1877–1931), National Liberal and later Liberal MP for Bristol South (1922–29).

8 'Politics in the West', *Cornubian and Redruth Times*, 26 October 1922, 4.

9 Algernon Moreing (1889–1974), Coalition Liberal MP for Buckrose (1918–22) and Camborne (1922–23), Constitutionalist and Conservative MP for Camborne (1924–29).

10 For Moreing's relationship with local Conservatives see minutes 1922–23 of the Conservative and Unionist Association (Cambourne Division), Kresen Kernow, X387.

11 'Revolt in East Dorset', *The Times*, 7 November 1922, 12.

12 'Independent Candidates', *Sheffield Daily Telegraph*, 3 November 1922, 7.

Chapter 6

Impact of the local elections and nomination day

The closing day for nominations was 4 November, and as it approached there was considerable nervousness at what might happen. Results day for the local elections was 2 November, with 1,362 candidates for just over 70 borough councils being elected; there was significant interest in their outcome, and what this might augur for the progress of the Labour Party or the effectiveness of local pacts in shutting out the socialists.[1] The *Western Morning News* for one was ready to conclude on 2 November that whatever the local election results showed, it was still 'improbable' that the Conservatives would be able to 'secure a working majority of the House'.[2] The *Daily Express* was rather more bullish, proclaiming: 'Labour routed everywhere'.[3]

Those results, which appeared in the national press on 3 November, were startling and appeared to confirm the apparent wisdom for both Conservative and Coalition Liberals in maintaining local pact arrangements. They also suggested that Liberal and Conservative voters were less apathetic than they had been in 1919 and had learned the lesson that Labour voters would turn out at the poll even if they did not. As *The Scotsman* informed its readers on 3 November the results had delivered 'an emphatic repudiation' to the holders of 'socialist doctrines'.[4] Of the almost 600 candidates which Labour had put forward for the local elections, almost two-thirds had been defeated.[5] Only in some of the larger industrial cities including Manchester, Birmingham, Sheffield and Derby, together with South Wales, did Labour appear able to resist the anti-socialist tide.

Table 6.1: 1922 local election results: Labour councillors in England and Wales

Council	Candidates	Successful	Defeated
Ashton-under-Lyne	8	0	8
Barnsley	11	3	8
Barrow	8	2	6
Bath	5	3	2
Birkenhead	10	1	9
Birmingham	19	8	11
Blackburn	9	3	6
Bolton	12	4	8
Bradford	21	9	12
Bristol	13	6	7
Burnley	10	1	9
Burton	4	2	2
Bury	2	1	1
Cardiff	13	3	10
Carlisle	3	2	1
Chesterfield	5	2	3
Colne	3	1	2
Coventry	12	1	11
Croydon	11	2	9
Darlington	4	3	1
Derby	13	6	7
Doncaster	4	2	2
Dudley	5	1	4
Ealing	1	0	1
East Ham	9	2	7
Exeter	4	2	2
Grimsby	5	2	3
Halifax	6	5	1
Huddersfield	9	1	8
Hull	6	1	5
Ipswich	8	4	4

Keighley	4	1	3
Kingston upon Thames	4	1	3
Leeds	12	5	7
Leicester	10	5	5
Leigh	5	3	2
Lincoln	6	3	3
Liverpool	18	1	17
Manchester	18	10	8
Merthyr Tydfil	7	6	1
Middlesbrough	4	2	2
Nelson	4	3	1
Newcastle upon Tyne	9	8	1
Newport	5	3	2
Northampton	10	1	9
Norwich	8	4	4
Nottingham	10	4	6
Oldham	8	1	7
Plymouth	13	1	12
Portsmouth	7	0	7
Preston	6	4	2
Reading	8	3	5
Richmond (Surrey)	3	0	3
Rotherham	5	2	3
Salford	12	5	7
Sheffield	17	9	8
Smethwick	5	3	2
Southampton	9	1	8
Southend-on-Sea	3	1	2
South Shields	10	7	3
St Helens	8	5	3
Stockport	9	3	6
Stoke-on-Trent	11	5	6

(*Continued*)

Table 6.1: Continued

Council	Candidates	Successful	Defeated
Sunderland	4	2	2
Swansea	15	9	6
Swindon	10	2	8
Wigan	9	5	4
Wolverhampton	8	3	5
Worcester	7	1	6
Total	574	215	359

In London, Labour suffered serious reverses in almost all boroughs. In Islington, for example, thirty-eight Labour councillors lost their seats to return a Labour group of just six on a council of sixty members. *The Scotsman* claimed 'a striking illustration of the advantages of co-operation between parties which differ to some extent on other matters, but are agreed in their opposition to Socialism'.[6]

Jubilation at the outcome of the result was widespread in both Conservative and Liberal ranks. *The Pall Mall Gazette* declared: 'Smashing defeat of Labour: Seats Lost Wholesale in London'.[7] The 'debacle' for Labour, with six London boroughs returning no Labour councillors, was put down to: 'the alliance which was established in many boroughs between the Municipal Reform and Progressive parties'.[8] Likewise in Scotland, a jubilant Liberal sympathiser, Lady Frances Balfour, wrote to her brother-in-law, former Conservative leader Arthur Balfour and Coalitionist, to express her satisfaction that in the local elections Labour had gained hardly anything.[9] For both *The Pall Mall Gazette* and Lady Balfour the local election results demonstrated the utility of maintaining party pacts.

The reverses to the Labour movement were particularly heartening to the forces of Coalition Liberalism. Many of the seats where Labour had fared badly, and where 'co-operation' had checked socialist hopes, covered constituencies where Coalition Liberal MPs were standing in the general election including seats in Lancashire covered by the Derby truce. The results in Bristol and Norwich were also a potential omen of good fortune for Coalition Liberal candidates in those areas.

The local election results provided a confirmation of the wisdom of maintaining party pacts into the election. Indeed, in the aftermath of the results, Herbert Morrison, the secretary and organiser of the London Labour

Party, paid tribute to 'the political machinery of the Coalition' and 'the anti-Labour Party' which had helped to deliver the results.[10] Nevertheless, as nomination day drew closer there was nervousness in National Liberal circles that Unionist Central Office might fall into line with Beaverbrook's personal campaign and spring a surprise and field a slate of Conservative candidates against former coalitionists. There might also have been some nervousness at the behaviour of some Coalition Liberal constituency parties. In Gloucester and in Hornsey, Coalition Liberal constituency parties declined to put forward a candidate and instead backed the Asquithian candidate.[11] The *Gloucester Journal* was happy to proclaim local Liberal reunification following a visit by Asquith to the constituency and the putting forward of a programme by the candidate that all Liberals could get behind.[12]

Notes

1 'London Day by Day', *Sheffield Daily Telegraph*, 1 November 1922, 6.

2 'Mr Lloyd George Angry', *Sheffield Daily Telegraph*, 1 November 1922, 7.

3 'Labour Routed Everywhere', *The Daily Express*, 2 November 1922, 1.

4 'Municipal Elections Augury', *The Scotsman*, 3 November 1922, 7.

5 'Great Socialist Rout', *Sheffield Daily Telegraph*, 3 November 1922, 7.

6 'Municipal Elections Augury', *The Scotsman*, 3 November 1922, 7.

7 'Smashing Defeat of Labour', *Pall Mall Gazette*, 2 November 1922, 1.

8 'Smashing Defeat of Labour', *Pall Mall Gazette*, 2 November 1922, 1.

9 Frances Balfour to Arthur James Balfour, 8 November 1922, 1st Earl of Balfour Papers, GD433/2/231/128, National Records of Scotland.

10 'Labour Fears', *Sheffield Daily Telegraph*, 3 November 1922, 7.

11 'London Notes', *Yorkshire Post and Leeds Intelligencer*, 10 November 1922, 8.

12 'Liberals Re-united in Gloucester', *Gloucester Journal*, 11 November 1922, 7.

Chapter 7

Defining Coalition Liberal strategy

On 2 November, McCurdy, Churchill and Fisher met to discuss the state of play in the election, with Churchill writing to Lloyd George the same day. The context of the meeting was that the truce between the Conservatives and Coalition Liberals was considered in danger of breaking down. A letter from Sir George Younger, reminding local Conservative Associations that the choice of whether to observe a local truce or not was up to them, was being interpreted in Liberal circles as giving free rein to the diehards to try and unseat sitting Coalition Liberals. *The Times* reported that as many as twenty-eight associations might bring forward candidates to break the local truce.

Younger's purpose, backed by the promise that Central Office would not endorse any candidate not backed by the local party, was the complete opposite of Liberal suspicions. The emergence of 'independent Conservative and Unionist' candidates, or some variation thereon, threatened the cohesion of the party just as much as it did the deal with the Coalition Liberals. Invariably these independents were from the right of the party, and there were plenty of centre-left Conservatives disturbed at the nature of their politics. For example, in Putney, the sitting Conservative Sammy Samuels, from a wealthy Iraqi-Jewish background, found himself opposed by an Independent Unionist in the form of Cyril Prescott-Decie, former Brigadier-General and a former Divisional Commissioner in the Royal Irish Constabulary until he had resigned over the government's Irish policy. His hard line on Irish Union seemingly extended to the rest of his politics, which prompted his intervention against a more 'liberal Conservative'. Efforts by Younger to get Prescott-Decie to go elsewhere came to nothing, which led to considerable irritation on the part of Lord Bearsted, the very wealthy and influential brother of Sammy Samuels. He expressed his considerable reluctance to give a large donation to campaign funds while his brother was subject to a diehard challenge. His letter showed that his concern went beyond the personal: 'If I am correctly informed these re-actionaries would set back the clock by centuries, re-establish religious disabilities and the inquisition if possible'.[1] Sir George Younger expressed his exasperation at the difficulties of keeping the party united in the face of unhelpful interventions in the election: 'Since we have got the Die Hards into our camp I have been doing my level best ... to get these internecine fights put a stop to'.[2] Bearsted, seemingly comforted by explanations that everything was being done that could be done, eventually relented and gave £1,000, but it was one of several issues demonstrating that from diehards on the right, to the out-and-out Coalitionists around Austen Chamberlain, party unity was constantly in question and that 'local arrangements' constituted the best hope of keeping the party together.

On the ground in the constituencies the emphasis on 'local arrangements' was not an automatic solution to the difficulties that they faced. In some cases there was pressure against local Conservatives standing behind the line of Central Office. For example, George Gibbs, leading Bristol Conservative and MP for Bristol West, wrote to Sir William Bull, to express has exasperation at the forces pulling against the Conservative–Coalition Liberal pact in the city. He said that in Bristol they had managed to preserve good relations with the Coalition Liberals, and that in each of the constituencies Lloyd George Liberals and Conservatives continued to support each other's efforts. However, recent speeches by Lloyd George and Lord Birkenhead, and internal party missives by George Younger, had strained local Conservative-Liberal relationships to the point that maintaining political harmony in the city was daily becoming more difficult, although at the moment all five candidates continued to stand by pledges to support a Bonar Law government.[3]

The problem with 'local arrangements' as a line of policy was that diehard Conservatives, as well as those more friendly to the idea of continuing co-operation with the Lloyd George Liberals, could interpret the instruction as favouring their own hopes and intentions, and Coalition Liberals in seats where a diehard challenge was under discussion lobbied Lloyd George to do something about the flagrant attempts to violate arrangements between the two parties. Variable responses to the call to stand by 'local arrangements' led Lloyd George to consider activating a reserve list of as many as 150 Coalition Liberal candidates to take the fight to the Conservatives.[4] The McCurdy, Churchill and Fisher meeting on 2 November was to consider whether to make this threat a reality, or whether some more limited response might be set in train.

With Coalitionists in both Conservative and Liberal ranks under pressure, on 2 November the *Yorkshire Evening Post* reported that Lloyd George had met with some of the former Coalition Liberal ministers to consider 'reprisals' against the Conservatives for opposing National Liberal candidates.[5] The reality of the 'reprisals' considered by Churchill was tempered by the realities of the political situation. Churchill argued that, in line with calculations by McCurdy, it was likely that the National Liberals would secure around 70–80 MPs and they would hold the balance of power in the new parliament.[6] In order to secure that number of MPs they would rely on Conservative voters supporting National Liberals in seats where local pacts remained in force. To field a larger number of candidates and to set up National Liberal challengers to Conservatives in seats already held by the Tories would invite reciprocal challenges in target seats for the National Liberals. Churchill doubted the wisdom of engaging in a wider war with their former coalition partners. Such a war would lose them goodwill and votes in those seats where party pacts held good, and the implicit threat of allowing Labour candidates to win in seats where the anti-socialist vote was split would damage the image of National Liberals. In any case, if stopping the electoral march of socialism was one of the goals of the party then it made no sense to court that as a potential outcome. A list of potential candidates, over and above those already nominated, to field against the Conservatives did exist but Churchill counselled that it should not be used (that list has not been located in the Scovell papers or in any other repository).

Churchill was, however, of the opinion that some action needed to be taken. He therefore indicated that on the morning of the next day Conservative Central Office should be approached and asked to provide a guarantee against the sudden emergence of anything other than a handful of extra prospective Conservative candidates in the election.[7] The quid pro quo would be that Coalition Liberal headquarters would provide a reciprocal guarantee against a flood of Lloyd George Liberal candidates suddenly being brought forward. Churchill had a good political relationship with Younger, who shortly before the Carlton Club meeting had confided in him that he was very perturbed that the Conservatives, as opposed to just a few diehards, were likely to be in complete revolt.[8] Indeed, Churchill and Younger, as fellow Scottish MPs, had worked together to manage some of the strains of the coalition within constituencies north of the border.[9] In the circumstances of the election Churchill probably felt that Younger would be willing to work with the National Liberals in order to avoid clashes that could only benefit the Labour Party.

There was good reason to suppose that Churchill's analysis was probably accurate. Although Younger was regarded as a diehard by many Coalition Liberals, and has generally been seen as one of the prime movers against the coalition, working with the likes of Stanley Baldwin, Samuel Hoare and some of the other Conservative junior ministers in 1922 to bring down the government in September-October, his political outlook was certainly more nuanced than simple Tory die-hardism. As party chairman from 1917, and working closely with Sir Robert Sanders, Conservative deputy chief whip, Younger had been deeply involved in the minutiae of the inner politics of the coalition. As a Scot he got on very well with Bonar Law until the latter stepped down as party leader in 1921. His relationship with Austen Chamberlain, as the new party leader, was marked by a deep suspicion that Lloyd George had him under his spell. In the midst of the 1922 General Election, Younger was only too well aware, as he monitored the appeal for campaign funds, that money in a 'pretty expensive election' was tight for Conservative donors and that minimising clashes between Conservatives and Coalition Liberals would help to keep costs down.[10] Reprisals and an escalating battle between former allies was not in the interests of either party.

It was unsurprising that some details of the prospect of 'reprisals' were seemingly leaked to the press (presumably by Lloyd George) even before the group of Liberal ministers met to consider it. The Coalition Liberal Party leadership was under pressure to respond to Conservative challenges in some constituencies in the south of England. Without some kind of counter-threat it appeared likely that other associations might break with local arrangements and field their own candidates against sitting Coalition Liberals. The need to leak the question of 'reprisals' in order to contain the threat from local Conservative Associations, and to provide some re-assurance to sitting Coalition MPs, can be seen in this excerpt from the *Western Morning News* on the day of the McCurdy, Churchill and Fisher meeting: 'So far no Conservative candidate put up to fight a Lloyd George Liberal has been withdrawn. Five of the ex-Premier's Administration are being opposed by

Conservatives, and a sixth may be included to-morrow'.[11] Tensions between the parties were leading to fractures within them, but it was hard for both the Conservatives and Coalition Liberals to address the tensions when they could not make their electoral strategy, and the likelihood of future close working arrangements between the two parties, clear to activists and the electorate.

Notes

1 Lord Bearsted to Lord Hylton, 30 October 1922, 3rd Baron Hylton Papers, Somerset Heritage Centre, DD/HY/15/5/31.

2 Young to Lord Hylton, 2 November 1922, 3rd Baron Hylton Papers, Somerset Heritage Centre, DD/HY/15/5/31.

3 George Gibbs to Sir William Bull, 2 November 1922, Bull Papers 5/6, Churchill College Cambridge.

4 'Mr Lloyd George Angry', *Sheffield Daily Telegraph*, 1 November 1922, 7.

5 'Reprisals Considered Improbable', *Yorkshire Evening Post*, 2 November 1922, 10.

6 Churchill to Lloyd George, 2 November 1922, CHAR2/125/50–53, Churchill Papers, Churchill College Cambridge.

7 Churchill to Lloyd George, 2 November 1922, CHAR2/125/50–53, Churchill Papers, Churchill College Cambridge.

8 Younger to Churchill, 14 October 1922, CHAR2/125/20, Churchill Papers, Churchill College Cambridge.

9 See for example the issue of East Perthshire, John Gilmour to Austen Chamberlain, 27 May 1922, CHAR2/122/159–164 and Austen Chamberlain to Winston Churchill, 16 June 1922, CHAR2/123/61, Churchill Papers, Churchill College Cambridge.

10 Younger to Lord Hylton, 2nd November 1922, 3rd Baron Hylton Papers, Somerset Heritage Centre, DD/HY/15/5/31.

11 'National Liberals Lament', *Western Morning News*, 2 November 1922, 4.

Chapter 8

Trying to broker a deal with the Conservatives

If Younger was approached on the morning of 3 November in line with Churchill's suggestion, then the most likely outcome was a polite refusal to enter into any sort of formal arrangement, combined with a reiteration that the party would continue to stand behind the agreed policy of honouring 'local arrangements' and discouraging local hostilities. On 2 November, the day before the meeting, with rumours circulating in London, Younger had given assurances of Conservative policy:

> Seen at the Unionist Headquarters in Westminster, last night, Sir George Younger dismissed the newspapers' assertions of his making a new attack on the National Liberals and Mr. Lloyd George retorting with a threat of open war at the polls. Sir George declared, 'There is not a word of truth in it. There has not been the slightest approach to a conference between Mr. McCurdy and me, and I have received no sort of message or ultimatum whatever from Mr. Lloyd George'. Sir Malcolm Fraser, the Unionist Chief Agent, agreed that the stories in the London evening papers took Unionist Headquarters by surprise, and that they knew nothing whatever to substantiate them. It was indicated that the Unionist Party would, in any event, continue its present policy of allowing local Unionist Associations to make local agreements with National Liberals if they chose, or to select their own candidates if they preferred. National Liberal Headquarters, nevertheless, stuck to their story that, 'there was a limited pact'.[1]

In the face of anything more formal, Coalition Liberals were left to put forward one or two 'new' candidates while hinting that a far larger number of candidates was waiting in the wings if the challenges to sitting Coalition Liberal MPs intensified. *The Times* reported that a hidden army of Lloyd George Liberal candidates was being held in reserve:

> It was declared last Monday that between one hundred and one hundred and fifty National Liberal candidates were being held in leash to let slip against Unionists if the Unionist attacks on Mr. Lloyd George's supporters were not sensibly diminished. Only two of the shadowy band revealed their whereabouts yesterday. One turned up in Shropshire [with the backing of both the Lloyd George and Asquith Liberals] to oppose Lord Windsor in the Ludlow Division. A second at Twickenham, where Sir William Joynson-Hicks, the new Parliamentary Secretary of the Overseas Trade Department, is seeking re-election. A careful estimate of the possibilities last night suggested that the hundred and fifty reserves would to-day dwindle to a skeleton force of eight or ten at most.[2]

The prospect of a wider war between Conservatives and Coalition Liberals sent ripples down to constituency level across the country prompting associations to re-examine their local arrangements. In Yorkshire, the *Sheffield Telegraph* openly inquired whether, in the event of all-out war between National Liberals and Conservatives, 'Sheffield Liberals [would] ... abide by their local understanding with local Unionists'.[3]

In an effort to quell such difficult questions in a speech in London on 4 November, with Lloyd George appearing with two Conservative ex-Ministers, the ex-premier went to great pains to emphasise, seemingly to Coalition Liberal Associations, but perhaps with one eye on the Conservatives: 'Where there is a pact between parties, abide by it honourably'.[4] Lloyd George's speech, after the rebuff from Younger, appears to have been an attempt to shore up the uneasy truce between the parties (by implication an appeal to play fair) in the run-up to the closing of nominations.

Notes

1 'National Liberals Lament', *Western Morning News*, 2 November 1922, 4.

2 'Strength of Parties – Nearly 1,400 Candidates – Ex–Premier's Hidden Army', *The Times*, 4 November 1922, 10.

3 'Mr Lloyd George Angry', *Sheffield Daily Telegraph*, 1 November 1922, 7.

4 'Ex-Premier on the Pacts', *The Times*, 6 November 1922, 10.

Chapter 9

Exchanges between the parties after 4 November

The threat of full scale hostilities between the parties does appear to have had some impact on the behaviour of Conservative associations. Further challenges to sitting Coalition Liberals did not materialise and Lloyd George's phantom army was not deployed. Indeed, in Twickenham the Coalition Liberal threat to oppose William Joynson-Hicks evaporated as quickly and mysteriously as it had appeared. In the aftermath of the close of nominations the newspapers and party leaderships attempted to make sense of where the parties stood in respect of each other and the likely outcome of the election. The *Sheffield Daily Telegraph* expressed satisfaction that Lloyd George had not jeopardised 'local arrangements' by 'producing his strategic reserve of candidates'.[1] Indeed, Lloyd George followed the close of nominations at Newcastle on 7 November when he said that he was ready to support any government wrestling with the problems of the peace. By this he clearly meant the Conservatives, as he went on to argue that his intention in securing the election of as many Liberals as possible was to save the government from 'Die-Hard extremists'.[2]

The truce, however, had not been maintained entirely. On 8 November the *Derby Daily Telegraph* revealed that Marshall Freeman (nominated in Ilkeston against the incumbent Coalition Liberal, General J. E. B. Seely) had received a letter of support from Bonar Law.[3] Matching Freeman's eleventh-hour candidature in Ilkeston, Derbyshire, was that of Henry Lorimer in South Derbyshire. The seat had been captured by Coalition Liberal Henry Gregory in 1918 with the benefit of the coupon but he was not standing again in 1922. His Labour opponent in 1918, Samuel Truman, was ready to stand again and the Coalition Liberals had decided to put forward a relatively unknown candidate, Goronwy Owen. That Owen had little to no connection to South Derbyshire, and was closely associated with Lloyd George's coterie of Welsh Coalition Liberals, alienated him from local supporters of Asquithian Liberalism, and persuaded local Conservatives to put forward their own candidate. Overall, the truce between the Conservatives and the Coalition Liberals had held, but in some circumstances local antagonisms were too strong to contain and Conservative Central Office felt that it had no choice but to support candidates legitimately put forward by local associations.

Notes

1 'The Nominations', *Sheffield Daily Telegraph*, 6 November 1922, 7.

2 'Lloyd George', *Dublin Evening Telegraph*, 7 November 1922, 1.

3 'The Premier and Ilkeston', *Derby Daily Telegraph*, 8 November 1822, 4.

Chapter 10

Methods and tone

A study of the methods of the 1922 election reveal a range of features common to modern British elections from well-established practices, such as the use of manifestos and election addresses, through to newer facets including the mass use of motor cars in campaigning, and the need to adapt campaign literature to the new democratic age. Much of the tone of what emerged through those methods reflected the rather strange circumstances of the 1922 general election, and the difficulties of the parties in coming to terms with the new methods and imperatives of campaigning.

The manifestos

If preserving the unofficial truce with the Coalition Liberals remained one of the goals of the Conservative Party leadership, and the party at the national level had carefully avoided tariff reform as a potential bone of contention, then the tone of the manifesto and every other election communication assumed an additional importance. While the Coalition Liberals could damn Bonar Law and his ministers with faint praise and references to wartime achievements and shared endeavours, for the Conservatives the central thrust of their manifesto and campaign (in line with the advice from the group of senior Tories asked to pronounce on the matter by Bonar Law) was that they would provide a government that would be sharply different in tone, methods and morals to that of Lloyd George. Conservative voters were left to infer how that would translate into policy towards government expenditure, foreign and colonial policy, and the domestic field. In addition, it did not stop newspapers from speculating on what a Conservative government might mean in spite of the apparent gaps in the manifesto.[1] The vacuum formed by the attempt to preserve a truce between the Conservatives and Coalition Liberals by having minimal disputes at the policy level was rapidly filled by differences, real and perceived, about what each party stood for.

In terms of the processes of realignment taking place within British politics, the significance of the policy vacuum in the 1922 election was underplayed by Maurice Cowling in *The Impact of Labour*.[2] If, in Cowling's eyes, the central achievement of the Conservative Party in the early 1920s was to define itself as chief opponent to socialism, and to define Labour as the principal party of opposition, then the Conservatives first had to disentangle themselves from the Coalition Liberals. The nature of the campaign in 1922 forced a process by which the electorate had to concentrate on perceptions of the core values of each party that had been buried from 1914 beneath the compromises and exigencies of a coalition to win the war. The lack of serious policy issues between the two former coalition partners effectively meant the contest between them was fought in terms of brand. For the Conservatives, that branding battle served to remind the electorate of the perceived traditional values of the Conservatives. For the Coalition Liberals the Lloyd George brand was badly tarnished in a number of respects, and the longer traditions which it could tap into were co-owned by the Asquith Liberals.

Their manifesto in turn made life harder for Liberals of both persuasions. Remarkably short and simple, the Asquith Liberal Party's manifesto had a first section headed 'Lloyd George and the Conservatives' in an attempt to ensure that those two parties remained firmly linked in the minds of voters. It wasn't until the third section that the manifesto began to detail a separate Liberal identity. Traditional Liberal values such as the defence of free trade, economy and the need to secure the populace against hardship were to the fore, but the latter was carefully coupled with assertions that 'Liberalism is not socialism. Liberalism repudiates the doctrine of warfare against private enterprise'.[3] While the Liberal manifesto contained a limited, and less than ringing, restatement of traditional Liberal values, it appeared, at the same time, to be remarkably unambitious. Underpinning it was a strong sense that the Asquith Liberals considered that the best they might achieve was to win sufficient seats to become the official opposition to the government. That, coupled with the adoption of proportional representation as a Liberal manifesto pledge, seemed to suggest that the Liberals under Asquith had almost given up on the idea of ever forming a government in their own right. As a restatement of the Liberal brand, the 1922 Asquith manifesto in tone and content left much to be desired.

Perhaps, however, a second game was being played out within the 1922 General Election. While the betting was on a Conservative-Coalition Liberal 'arrangement' after the election, it was not wholly out of the question that Bonar Law might seek to do a deal with Asquith, or at least to keep the prospect in play in order to potentially head off Asquith's support for a Labour minority government. The likely poll outcomes under discussion in late October pointed to a number of possible permutations by which a government might be arrived at. In forming his government following his acceptance of the premiership, Bonar Law had asked Reginald McKenna, former Liberal chancellor of the exchequer then serving as chairman of the Midland Bank, to return to his old post. While the appointment of a bank chairman to the exchequer might please the City, the move appeared to be more about sending a message to the Asquith Liberals. McKenna preferred not to take up the offer of the exchequer, fearing for his post at the bank, but strikingly during the campaign McKenna came out for Bonar Law even though he remained a Liberal.[4] The less than powerful restatement of the Liberal brand in the manifesto may have been Asquith similarly leaving the door open to co-operation with a Bonar Law ministry.

The Labour Party manifesto, by contrast, and useful in terms of pushing other parties towards coalitionism, was far more ambitious, promising changes to taxation to make the burden of public expenditure fairer while emphasising its concern for sensible economy that was not 'penny wise' but pound foolish. Housing and industry were central to the Labour Party programme, but the concerns of the agricultural sector (both farmers and labourers) was also highlighted. The manifesto highlighted Labour's socialist credentials while suggesting that the party was the best way to chart a middle course between the twin dangers of reaction and revolution. The Labour manifesto suggested a party that was moderate and modern, rooted in traditional British values while eschewing the political extremes: a party that could represent the aspirations of the working-class base (industrial/urban and rural) of British society. There was enough in the manifesto, however, for anti-socialists to use it to their advantage and to maintain a united front against Labour.

Local candidates

To some extent these branding issues fed through into the election addresses of candidates. Typically published in the local press, they varied widely in their nature from point-by-point iterations of policy through to more informal letters to constituents. This diversity may, in part, be a reflection of the state of the party machines at the outbreak of the campaigns. As John Ramsden notes, the election caught the Conservative Party cold: '[Overall] Party organisation played little part in the campaign. Virtually no literature was available at the outset for nobody knew a month before polling day on what basis the election would be fought'.[5] Nevertheless, some individual associations, such as at Lincoln, had to some extent been energised by election chatter in late 1921–early 1922 and were better placed to respond to the challenge of a quick campaign.[6] Meanwhile the Labour Party machine was fully geared up for the campaign. As F. M. Leventhal notes, from 1918 onwards the administration of the Labour Party was in the very 'capable hands' of Arthur Henderson. His 'knowledge of the party apparatus, and especially of local activists and constituency politics, made him indispensable'. The outcome of the general election would result in a vindication of the 'party machine' under Henderson.[7] While the Conservative campaign would rely, perhaps a little too heavily, on local efforts, Labour was ready with a profusion of campaign literature. Likewise, the Liberals of both varieties were prepared to spend heavily. All parties appreciated that election literature, even if produced to a common template, had to be carefully tailored to local requirements. The diversity was nevertheless dizzying.

In Exeter, the address by the Conservative candidate (Sir Robert Newman)[8] was in the form of a letter which he signed off 'Your obedient servant'.[9] In Hammersmith South, another Conservative, Sir William Bull, who had voted against ending the coalition at the Carlton Club, proclaimed that he would abide by the will of the majority of the party in breaking away from the coalition.[10] His coalitionist leanings were, however, well known even to the point of chairing a meeting in his constituency in support of Lloyd George. *The Times* had some sympathy, remarking: 'He dreads disunion in current circumstances: He believes in peace'.[11]

In Bristol East, Harold Morris,[12] the Coalition Liberal candidate, put out his election address in the local newspapers on 7 November. He was careful to emphasise that he was endorsed by both the Coalition Liberal and

Conservative associations in the constituency. Strikingly, the focus for much of his address revolved around foreign policy with support for the League of Nations and the payment of just reparations by Germany. On economic issues he backed prudent government economies, free trade, support for unemployed ex-servicemen and moderate trade unions. He also voiced his support for housing, health and education initiatives. Echoing the party line he wrote: 'Re-action represents hopeless stagnation – revolution complete submersion – neither has any place in my political convictions'.[13] Notably he also reminded his readers of his own wartime service (he'd served with the Coldstream Guards during the war) with a nod to the fact that the anniversary of the armistice would fall during the election: 'I have seen the bare and desolated plains of France and Flanders during and since the war'.[14]

In terms of content Morris's election address differed little from some of the Conservative candidates facing a strong challenge from Labour and hoping to enlist Liberal support. In Nottingham Rushcliffe, Henry Betterton[15] had won the seat for the Conservatives with the benefit of the coupon in 1918. Facing a straight fight against Labour, his election address had some warm words for the coalition as a vital necessity in the aftermath of the war. Support for ex-servicemen, easing unemployment, a foreign policy based around the League of Nations and anti-socialism were the pillars of his election address.[16]

In some constituencies, where Conservatives were looking for support from Liberals, election addresses emphasised respect for Lloyd George, his war record and the coalition. For example, in Birmingham (Handsworth) Oliver Locker Lampson,[17] Austen Chamberlain's parliamentary private secretary from 1919 to 1922 (transferring from a seat in Huntingdonshire), faced a challenge from a well-known and respected local independent. Lampson was careful to solicit support on a wide basis: 'The Coalition has vanished, and with it the leadership of Mr. Lloyd George, whose services in the Great War were magnificent and should never be forgotten. I had hoped to fight this Election, even as we fought the War, in close co-operation with allies from every side. But this has become impossible, and I am now called upon to contest this seat as a Unionist'.[18]

In the Plymouth Drake constituency, newly created in 1918, Conservative Arthur Shirley Benn looked for support from Coalition Liberals to reinforce his position against Labour and Asquithian Liberal challengers. His election address referred to the feeling 'by many people that a Conservative and Unionist Administration (with the co-operation of many Liberals) will deal in a more business like way with some of the many difficult subjects which are facing us'.[19] His four key policy points emphasising the importance of private enterprise, opposition to nationalisation, lowering taxation, and opposition to the capital levy suggested a platform that most Liberals could support.

The profusion of campaign literature in Shoreditch for Dr Christopher Addison was particularly noteworthy, emphasising the costliness of the election and the way in which national campaign messaging could come second to local circumstances shaped by particular candidates and issues. One of Lloyd George's ministers, until a growing estrangement between the two reached its culmination in 1921, Addison stood again for the Shoreditch constituency which he had represented since 1910. The difference was that in 1922 he was standing as one of Asquith's Liberals. Believing that the Coalition Liberal organisation was determined to get him, Addison fought a remarkably vigorous campaign in which an absolute welter of election campaign material was produced along the lines of 'Shoreditch needs the Doctor', reminding voters of his reputation as a campaigner for health and social reform.[20] The cost of his campaign was considerable: over £1,250 including £252 on campaign literature and posters, not including delivery.[21] Posters large, small and window-size proliferated, including a flyer the size and shape of a beer mat as Addison spent to the maximum allowed campaign expenses equating to 5 pence per elector under the 1883 Corrupt and Illegal Practices Prevention Act.[22] At every turn Addison's campaign literature identified him with some of the achievements of the Lloyd George government when he was Minister of Health from 1919 to 1921, while trying to situate him as a firm opponent of the coalition: a man of the people (particularly the working class) but without being too radical. The breach between Addison and Lloyd George was identified as the latter's willingness to spend money on Britain's emergent Middle Eastern empire that might have been better used to address the needs of the working classes. It was a difficult balancing act to pull off, as he attempted to appeal to Liberal, Labour and, to a certain extent, Conservative voters, and ultimately it was to prove unsuccessful as he did indeed lose to the Lloyd George Liberal, Ernest Price.

The file on Shoreditch in Addison's papers at the Bodleian Library indicates that his Labour and National Liberal opponents did their best to respond to the productivity and creativeness of the local Liberal campaign. Ernest Price's campaign identified Addison with the 'squandermania' of the postwar period, while the Labour candidate suggested that he, rather than Addison, was the real 'People's Man' with a 'People's Programme'.[23] The upshot would, however, be that 'The Doctor' would find himself out of Westminster, financially embarrassed by his levels of campaign spending, hounded by his agent for hundreds of pounds, and having to appeal to party grandees for financial support, as he dispensed with his servants and made economies at home.[24]

To some extent the central parties could help candidates within their constituencies. The Labour Party Press Bureau, for example, used a standardised form to gather information from all candidates so that it could provide short pen-portraits of its prospective parliamentary candidates to the local and national media. Notes on candidates tended to emphasise the union/activist credentials of candidates, their religious and humanitarian work, together with service during the First World War.[25] Likewise the central party turned out a veritable blizzard of publicity with thirteen million leaflets being produced during the general election, six new posters designed, and ten million copies of the manifesto printed.[26] At the same time, Labour's Joint Research and Information Party provided useful intelligence to candidates on their opponents, including the directorships which they held.[27]

The extent to which local candidates were able to mediate the central branding of the party is difficult to quantify, especially when centrally produced campaign literature, and memos (in the case of the Conservatives), informed and guided candidates and agents.[28] Strikingly, with the locally produced campaign literature, most emphasised a select few of the promises made by the central parties in terms of manifesto and speeches by major figures within the party. Others contained appeals for cross-party support in line with local party truces and the unofficial ceasefire between two of the parties. Noteworthy, like those in support of Addison's campaign, were those addresses which emphasised the personal qualities and previous service of the candidate in the hopes of developing cross-party support. Perhaps the ultimate expression of this kind of localism came with the candidature of Edgar Chatfeild-Clarke, for the Asquith Liberals on the Isle of Wight. Beyond his support for traditional Liberal values, the principal selling point of his campaign was that as a fifth-generation islander, from a well-known island family, he was 'the real island man', rather than some party hopeful parachuted in from somewhere else.[29] Being a true islander ('A Lifetime Islander for the Island')[30] was presented to the electorate as an issue which trumped all others, including a party label. In the case of the Isle of Wight, local identity in the campaign could eclipse national issues.

Getting the message over

The strategies of particular candidates, either standing firmly behind central manifesto and messaging, emphasising the party brand, promoting particular issues of relevance to the constituency, appealing for cross-party support or highlighting the personal qualities of the candidate, were further repeated in public meetings. These meetings were held across constituencies, often two per day in the evenings after work. The favoured venues were parish halls and schools but also included street corners and selected businesses during working hours. For example, the speaking engagements for Colonel C. H. C. Guest (Coalition Liberal) in North Bristol included:

7 November – 8 p.m. address at Greenbank Council School;
8 November – 1.50 p.m. address at Messrs Fox's works and 8 p.m. at St. Simon's School;
9 November – 8 p.m. address at Chester Park Council School;
10 November – 8 p.m. address at Horley Road Council School;
11 November – 12.30 p.m. address at corner of Harleston Street, 1.15 p.m. at Reading Road and 8 p.m. at Ashley Down Council Schools;
13 November – 1.15 p.m. address at Picton Street, 7.30 p.m. at St. Thomas's Parish Hall, 8 p.m. at Stapleton Memorial Hall;
14 November – 1.15 p.m. address at Sussex Place, 7.30 p.m. at Fishponds Parish Hall, 8 p.m. at Old Library Premises, Trinity Road.[31]

The parties prepared their candidates for these public events to varying degrees with the Labour Party organisation proving particularly effective. David Marquand notes that in Aberavon, eventual Labour victory did not rest too heavily on the 'exalted oratory' of Ramsay MacDonald at meetings but on 'careful planning', preparation and organisation and a network of 'polling district committees'.[32] The Labour Speakers Handbook, priced at one shilling, provided comprehensive responses on almost any given issue across its 161 pages covering 39 topics, with a detailed index for easy reference and speed of reply, and in a long, thin envelope style for convenient carrying in an inner pocket. Its domestic topics included finance, Labour and the rates, taxation of land values, unemployment, trades unions and trade boards. Answers on foreign, imperial and military affairs were also provided with sections on disarmament, India, reparations, Egypt, Russia and Ireland. Several sections covering such things as maternity and pensions for women and children were targeted very much at women voters. Noteworthy was the fact that during the campaign, addenda and updates to the handbook were issued (at least ninety-four) by the central party to respond to areas of particular interest or where the lines taken by other parties necessitated a change or an adjustment of emphasis.[33] Just as important was a foreword by Arthur Henderson, the chief whip, that emphasised that Labour was no longer simply the party of the working classes, but rather it strove for a new order in the 'human interest'.[34] This was 'effective fighting ammunition' for a party trying to reach out beyond its core base to the middle classes.[35]

Life on the stump for candidates in urban areas offered considerable challenges of organisation and timing. Meetings in urban areas could run into surprising problems, especially in securing venues. At the outset of his campaign Christopher Addison in Shoreditch allocated £35.00 for booking meeting venues but still found it difficult to find suitable premises as so many schools were booked out after 5 p.m. for London County Council evening classes.[36]

Meanwhile in the rural areas large distances had to be traversed often in the interest of addressing just a handful of people in remote villages. The use of a car was all but essential in the more rural areas. For example, in the Tiverton constituency where Herbert Sparkes was the hopeful Conservative candidate, the distances involved in a large rural constituency called for military precision to facilitate speaking appearances in the organisation of meetings in some of the smaller villages. The diary of his wife, preserved in the Devon Record Office, contains some loose pages providing the evening speaking itinerary for her husband in early November. By grouping particular villages together (separated by two to five miles), and by utilising support speakers to hold the fort, or round off, it was possible to hop from one meeting to another by car, across a two-hour period making a starring performance before moving on to the next event.[37]

To support how these election events were reported the Labour Party Press Bureau went out of its way to make the life of the political journalist that bit easier, and to shape the way that the activities of their candidates were seen. For the benefit of the press, Labour maintained a central collection of candidates' mini-biographies, drawn up by means of a form, to shape and humanise how candidates might be reported in the newspapers.[38] To the fore in the reports was trade union work, wartime experiences, church and public service.[39] This provided some human context to the campaign material and election meetings.

The visual look

The growing influence of the visual medium, including newsreels, made itself felt on the 1922 General Election. While the politicians had a good understanding of platform rhetoric and written appeals to the electors, just how did they combine this with an understanding of visual media to help convey their message? Beyond a display of rosettes with party colours, election rallies lacked the kind of branding and visual signifiers that became steadily more present in twentieth-century elections. In some cases, a lack of understanding of the visual message led to some curious choices. For example, for Bonar Law's appearance in front of a women's rally the set dressers at the Drury Lane theatre arranged for a painted backdrop of a medieval cathedral which unfortunately made him look in the eyes of one correspondent like 'a stained-glass martyr'.[40] Large placards carrying the name of the candidate and invocation to vote for them were also a feature of the election common to various parties. The messages were usually simple, 'Horne for Hillhead', ran those for Conservative Robert Horne in Glasgow.[41] Sometimes the messages were more complex. In East Edinburgh for example, ex-soldier Colonel Sam MacDonald for the Coalition Liberals ran placards proclaiming: 'MacDonald fought for you in Flanders; Send Him to Fight for you in Westminster'.[42] In the case of the Coalition Liberals, placards might display an image of Lloyd George with the message to vote National Liberal. In Bonar Law's Glasgow Central constituency one particularly interesting placard featured an image of a bearded Russian. Underneath it read: 'He wants you to vote Socialist. Don't'.[43] Placards were considered particularly effective when they could be placed on the side of a motor car. Perhaps lacking the funding of the other party, Labour Party supporters (and occasionally those of other parties) sometimes used chalk to create their own pavement placards in support of their candidates.

Election addresses frequently carried images of the candidates in either their best clothes or, for ex-servicemen, in uniform. In Birmingham, Handsworth the election leaflet for Oliver Locker Lampson DSO (Royal

Navy Volunteer Reserve), carried a head and shoulders image of him in service dress.[44]

The Labour Party included sketch images to supplement many of its election leaflets. For example, an image of two men talking with a church in the background accompanied the leaflet 'Job's Talks: Voting Labour'.[45] With the 'patience of Job' the leaflet details the conversation as a Labour candidate convinces John Smith (the carpenter) to vote Labour as the only party that will do anything for him. The image of the church backed by religious allusions in the text (Job from the Old Testament and the ordinary voter who shares with Jesus Christ the profession of carpenter) turn a political pamphlet into a neo-religious tract. Further pamphlets were produced in the 'Job's Talks' series, still using the same imagery and making a similar pitch which dealt with 'Unemployment', 'Housing' and 'Lower Taxes for the Workers'. A variation on the pamphlet with an appropriately re-worked sketch, still with the church as the background, was produced advising 'Why women should vote Labour'.[46] Sketch-like images could also be found on pamphlets such as 'What's Life Like on [*sic*] the Countryside' [a fearful and poverty stricken elderly couple], and 'To the Woman in the Home' (mother washing the dishes with a child at her side).[47] These simply produced images reinforced some of the central message of the campaign literature.

At a higher level of production values, and artistic quality, stood a standardised candidate flyer entitled 'The Labour Policy is the People's Policy'.[48] On the front cover an image of the local candidate (which was changed for each constituency), was set in a box, against a background of two other images (a man working at a lathe and a factory worker gazing to the new dawn in the distance), evocative of the kind of socialist art seen typically in union banners. Inside were images of family life in the form of simple line drawings, reminiscent of 'Job's Talks' that supported the text of the flyer under the captions 'No Food Taxes' and 'Houses for the People'.

Labour reached its highest level of artistic ambition with Labour leaflet No. 44. The leaflet entitled 'The Endless Chain' reproduced English painter C. R. W. Nevinson's (1889–1946) 1917 lithograph entitled 'Loading the Ship'.[49] Drawing on cubist, vorticist and futurist influences, and his experiences of painting the horrors of trench warfare, Nevinson's image showed men labouring under the weight of heavy burdens. Strikingly it was coupled with a poem by English writer Eleanor Farjeon (1881–1965). The leaflet made no overt political point but the image, combined with a poem that evoked the idea of men as the flesh and bone parts of a machine in perpetual motion, was clear in its sympathies.

For the Labour Party the different types of imagery at play in some of the election material, from simple portrait photographs, to images inspired by religious tracts, the trade union movement, and the latest currents in European Art and culture, seem to have been arrived at accidentally rather than as part of a concerted policy to produce different kinds of campaign literature to appeal to different sections of the electorate. The diversity reflected the character of a Labour Party which by 1922 encapsulated the middle-class graduates of the Fabian society through to those whose place of learning was the factory floor and the chapel.

Throughout the election the volume of printed material produced for the voter was considerable. One commentator wrote:

> 'Never has there been such a flood of appeals to the electors on paper. The output of the Conservatives totalled fifty tons, including nineteen million leaflets and three hundred thousand posters. Labour sent out forty tons, the leaflets alone numbering eighteen millions. The Independent Liberals distributed thirty tons, the leaflets numbering fifteen millions; and the National Liberals ten tons, including four million leaflets'.[50]

The women's vote

All parties recognised the importance of the women's vote following the enfranchisement of women over thirty in the 1918 election. In some constituencies it was especially important because, despite the unequal franchise, women constituted the majority of registered electors. Cheltenham was one such constituency with women voters (12,052) marginally outnumbering male voters (11,925).[51] How to garner their votes in 1922 exercised the party leaderships, agents and constituency workers. The Conservative approach was not to treat women differently and to refuse to acknowledge that there might be such things as 'womens' issues' that might be targeted by particular means. For example, at several points during the campaign Bonar Law spoke to rallies of women voters, but rhetorically he was at pains to suggest that, while women and men might have a slightly different outlook, they were united on the issues. He considered

> 'women were a little more cautious, a little less inclined to try rash experiments than men … [but that this] was an element which would strengthen and not weaken the Constitution of a country like ours. (Cheers.) He had no special message for women – indeed, had not two ways of speaking at all. He addressed all audiences – as he did in the House of Commons – as reasonable human beings'.[52]

Despite his protestations of gender-blindness, Bonar Law nevertheless sent a letter for publication and circulation as a pamphlet to Viscountess Caroline Bridgeman (1864–1935) in her role as chair of the Conservative Women's Organisation (CWO). The CWO had been officially founded in 1919 (though it would not be formally affiliated to the party until 1928) as a grassroots organisation to provide a focus for Conservative women and as a means to capture the women's vote. In the letter Bonar Law proclaimed 'I have been a consistent supporter of women's suffrage', and made reference to 'all the special questions in which they are particularly interested'.[53]

The eagerness with which women embraced the campaign of 1922 can be glimpsed in an address given by Bonar Law to a 'packed' women's only audience at the Drury Lane theatre in London on Thursday 2 November.[54] More than 2,250 women packed the theatre to hear Bonar Law give a speech that was heavy on foreign policy issues. The remarkable thing is that more than 8,000 had applied for tickets.[55] One correspondent gave a detailed reading of the performance, praising Bonar Law for addressing his audience not as women but 'as citizens, nay more, as though they were acute and trained politicians on the floor of the House of Commons'. The correspondent praised Bonar Law for not simply trying to appeal to women on the basis of the cost of living ('threepenny loaf and tea at 1s. 2d.), or of making emotional appeals like Lloyd George on the basis of '"sob stuff" about the horrors of war, the anguish of bereaved mothers and his own mission to ensure peace'.[56]

Some constituencies during the election saw the holding of women-only meetings by candidates in addition to mixed-sex open meetings. Such meetings were, in part, a recognition of the practicalities of childcare with women perhaps unable to attend evening meetings because of the need to get children fed and into bed after school. They were a particular feature of the campaign run by Harold Morris for the Coalition Liberals in East Bristol. His campaign engagements included:

7 November – 3 p.m. address at St Michael's Parish Hall (Women Only), 7 p.m. St. Silas School, 8 p.m. at St Anne's Council School;
8 November – 7 p.m. address at Avonvale Road Council, 8 p.m. at St Gabriel's School;
9 November – 3 p.m. address at St Mark's Lecture Hall (Women Only), 7.30 p.m. Bedfield Council School, 8.00 p.m. Crew's Hole Methodist School;
10 November – 3 p.m. address at St Matthew's Parish Hall (Women Only), 8 p.m. St. Michael's Parish Hall.[57]

Some of these attempts to engage the woman voter were almost comic in their lack of engaging content. The women voters of the Liverpool Exchange division were treated to a lengthy oration (his draft speech ran for thirty-six pages) by Sir Leslie Scott that consisted entirely of a close reading of Labour Party policy and a detailed analysis of the evils and contradictions of socialism. Conservative Party policy was not mentioned and only at the end of his paper did the Conservative Coalitionist reach his punchline and his point: that the two main parties in Britain had no right to let the Labour Party get its hands on power.[58]

Elsewhere candidates attempted to engage women voters on a more relatable level. In Shoreditch, for example, Dorothy Thurtle, the wife of the Labour candidate, assured the women voters of the constituency that her husband had 'many faults (all husbands have!) but I think I can truthfully say that he is honest and sincere, and, if elected, will fight your battles to the best of his ability'.[59] Wrapped around with assurances that she was an East End woman, Mrs Thurtle's intervention was disarmingly charming.

Only a handful of associations were prepared to run what they saw as the perceived risk of having a woman candidate on the ballot, but they did incite considerable press interest, including from the *Daily Mirror*, which carried photographs of three of the candidates on its front page on 30 October.[60] By nomination day twenty-six women candidates had been put forward in the constituencies: a moderate increase on the seventeen who had stood in 1918, and many of them were considered 'safe' candidates. Some eight of them, like Nancy Astor elected in 1919, had aristocratic connections and could be considered to be from known political backgrounds.

Elsewhere, the wives of male candidates were prepared to do their bit to get the female vote out in support of their husbands. In the Birmingham Ladywood constituency, 'Mrs Neville Chamberlain' advised women voters to vote for her husband because she knew that he had their interests at heart.[61]

At every turn, women were making their presence felt in the election, but the parties were still very much feeling their way as to how to capitalise on the woman's vote.

Disruption of election meetings

In some areas the behaviour of Labour supporters probably did much to reinforce the perceived need for a party pact. In Dundee, Churchill experienced a particularly brutal reception from left-wing and Irish elements determined to prevent him from speaking. As William Walker has noted, faced with a determined effort to disrupt his campaign, the Churchill campaign 'could neither understand nor effectively counter it'.[62] Churchill was not the only one to meet such hostility, with the *Yorkshire Post and Leeds Intelligencer* condemning the 'hooliganism of the Socialist-Communists' being visited on Sir Alfred Yeo in Poplar, a noted hotbed of civic Labourism, and in other constituencies including Norwich, Penryn and Falmouth.[63] In the Glasgow Bridgeton Division, Alexander MacCallum Scott,[64] chief whip for the Scottish Coalition Liberals, responded forcefully by calling meetings in which he expounded the principles of Marxism before pulling them apart for the benefit of his audience.[65]

In some cases, quick-witted responses could still win difficult audiences. For example, in the Southampton constituency where two Coalition Liberals who had first won the seat in 1906 were facing a challenge from the Conservatives and Labour, local dockers gave Tory speakers a hard time. The Duke of Northumberland, with his mining connections, was given a particularly difficult reception. Fortunately, also with him on the platform was the Australian singer Nellie Melba. As she spoke in favour of the Conservative candidates she was heckled with a cry of 'Give us a song, Nellie'.[66] She retorted by saying that she would, but only if the audience listened to her afterwards. The crowd roared back 'We will'. Taking to the piano on stage she sang 'Home Sweet Home' before going on to praise the Conservative candidates as honourable men, loyal to the cause of Empire.

Notes

1 'Mr Bonar Law's Manifesto', *Western Morning News*, 27 October 1922, 4.

2 Maurice Cowling, *The Impact of Labour, 1920–1924*, 213–36.

3 Liberal Party Manifesto 1922, http://www.libdemmanifesto.com/1922/1922-liberal-manifesto.shtml accessed 25 June 2020.

4 'Mr McKenna', 26 October 1922, British Pathé Film Archive, Film Id.286.27

5 Ramsden, *The Age of Balfour and Baldwin, 1902–1940*, 170.

6 Secretary's Annual Report for 1921, Conservative and Unionist Association (Lincoln Division), Lincoln Record Office, Misc Don1095/1/1/1.

7 F. M. Leventhal, *Arthur Henderson* (Manchester: Manchester University Press, 1989), 101.

8 Sir Robert Newman (1871–1945), Conservative/Independent Conservative MP for Exeter (1918–31).

9 'Exeter Parliamentary Election', *Western Morning News*, 31 October 1922, 1.

10 Sir William Bull election address, 1 November 1922, Bull Papers 5/6, Churchill College Cambridge.

11 'Contests for West London', *The Times*, 6 November 1922, 14.

12 Harold Morris (1876–1967), Coalition Liberal MP for Bristol East 1922–23.

13 'To the Electors of Bristol East', *Western Daily Press*, 7 November 1922, 4.

14 'To the Electors of Bristol East', *Western Daily Press*, 7 November 1922, 4.

15 Henry Betterton, 1st Baron Rushcliffe (1872–1949), Conservative MP for Rushcliffe (1918–34), Minister of Labour 1931–4.

16 'Election Address', *South Notts Echo*, 11 November 1922, 4.

17 Oliver Locker Lampson (1880–1954), Coalition Conservative and later Conservative MP for Huntingdonshire (1918–22), Handsworth, Birmingham (1922–45).

18 'Oliver Locker Lampson election address, 1922', Birmingham Parliamentary Elections 1918–22, LFF76.8 (14/5521), Local Studies and History Department, Birmingham Central Library.

19 'Election Address', *Western Morning News*, 8 November 1922, 1.

20 'Shoreditch needs the Dr', campaign poster, Bodleian Library, MS Addison dep. C.197 f97.

21 'Estimate of election expenses', Bodleian Library, MS Addison dep. C.197 f207.

22 'Addison', campaign literature, Bodleian Library, MS Addison dep. C.197 f143.

23 'A Vote for Price' and 'Vote for Thurtle the Labour Party Candidate', Bodleian Library, MS Addison dep. C.197 ff100–104.

24 See Addison to Lord Gladstone, 13 December 1922, Bodleian Library, MS Addison dep. C.197 ff241–242.

25 'Biographical Notices of Labour Candidates', Labour Party Archive, LP/ELEC/1922/1.

26 Report of the 23rd Annual Conference, 42, Labour Party Archive, People's History Museum.

27 See, for example, 'Croft', Brig. Gen. Henry Page' GE1922 No. 22, Labour Party Archive, LP/ELEC/1922/1.

28 For the 1922 General Election nine memos were produced (this would rise to thirty-nine in 1923). For the 1922 General Election see for example, 'Labour Party's Election Manifesto', 'Mr Bonar Law and the Capital Levy', 'Labour Party's Agricultural Policy', 'War Pensions Answered', Conservative Party Archive: Printed and Published Material: General Election Memos, CPA PUB456 1 ff1–27.

29 'Binstead Drill Hall', *Isle of Wight Observer*, 11 November 1922, 2.

30 'Isle of Wight Parliamentary Election Card for Sir Edgar Chatfeild-Clarke', Isle of Wight Record Office, AC2019/7.

31 'North Bristol Parliamentary Election', *Western Daily Press*, 7 November 1922, 4.

32 Marquand, *Ramsay MacDonald*, 281.

33 See, for example, Joint Research and Information Department's notes on 'Roman Catholic Schools', General Election [Hereafter GE1922] 1922 No. 3a, 'Tory War Policy', GE1922 No. 4, 'Unemployment', GE1922 No. 5, 'Housing', GE1922 No. 10, 'Notes on Labour Party Manifesto Regarding Taxation', GE1922 No. 18, 'The Conservatives and Military Alliances', GE1922 No. 94, Labour Party Archive, LP/ELEC/1922/1.

34 Foreword by Arthur Henderson, *The Labour Speaker's Handbook* (London: Labour Party, 1922), p.v. Labour Party Archive, LP/ELEC/1922/1.

35 *Labour Speaker's Handbook*, p.v., Labour Party Archive, LP/ELEC/1922/1.

36 'Estimate of campaign expenses', 19 October 1922, Bodleian Library, MS Addison dep. C.197 f207.

37 Loose pages in Emily Sparkes Diary, November 1922, Devon Record Office SPA/F/2/32.

38 Form 'General Election Publicity Campaign', Labour Party Archive, LP/ELEC/1922/1.

39 Biographical notices of Labour candidates, Labour Party Archive, LP/ELEC/1922/1.

40 'London Day by Day', *Sheffield Daily Telegraph*, 3 November 1922, 6.

41 'Scenes in Glasgow', *The Scotsman*, 16 November 1922, 6.

42 'East Division', *The Scotsman*, 16 November 1922, 6.

43 'The Premier's Constituency', *The Scotsman*, 16 November 1922, 6.

44 'Oliver Locker Lampson election address, 1922', Birmingham Parliamentary Elections 1918–22, LFF76.8 (14/5521), Local Studies and History Department, Birmingham Central Library.

45 'Job's Talks', Labour Party Archive, LP/ELEC/1922/1.

46 'Mrs Job's Talks', Labour Party Archive, LP/ELEC/1922/1.

47 'What's Life Like on the Countryside', Labour Party Archive, LP/ELEC/1922/1.

48 'The Labour Policy is the People's Policy', copies for E. Picton-Tuberville (Islington North), J. W. Bowen (Newport), Charles G. Ammon (Camberwell North), H. W. Wallace (Bury), Labour Party Archive, LP/ELEC/1922/1. For G. Ammon in 1922 see volume of press cuttings relating to Lord Ammon, Vol. 1, 1920–1922, Ammon Papers, Hull History Centre. U DMN/3/1.

49 'The Endless Chain', Labour leaflet No. 44, Labour Party Archive, LP/ELEC/1922/1.

50 'A Flood of Literature', *The Western Morning News and Mercury*, 16 November 1922, 4.

51 'Contest in Cheltenham', *Gloucestershire Echo*, 15 November 1922, 6.

52 'General Election Polls Today', *Belfast News-Letter*, 15 November 1922, 5.

53 Bonar Law to Mrs Bridgeman, 8 November 1922, Bridgeman papers, Shropshire Archives, X4629/1/1922/359/1.

54 'Prime Minister's Great Meeting for Women', *Daily Mirror*, 3 November 1922, 1.

55 'Disraeli's Aim', *Sheffield Daily Telegraph*, 3 November 1922, 7.

56 'London Day by Day', *Sheffield Daily Telegraph*, 3 November 1922, 6.

57 'Bristol East Parliamentary Division', *Western Daily Press*, 7 November 1922, 4.

58 Typescript Address by Sir Leslie Scott to Women Voters in his Constituency (undated), Scott Papers, Modern Records Centre, University of Warwick, MSS.119/3/S/LI/16.

59 'A word from Mrs Thurtle', Bodleian Library, MS Addison dep. C.197 f102.

60 '29 Woman Candidates', *The Daily Mirror*, 30 October 1922, 1.

61 Anne Chamberlain to the electors of Ladywood and Rotton Park, 11 November 1922, Neville Chamberlain papers, NC5/12/16.

62 William M. Walker, 'Dundee's Disenchantment with Churchill: A Comment upon the Downfall of the Liberal Party', *The Scottish Historical Review* 49, no.147, Pt. 1 (1970), 85–108 (107).

63 'National Liberals Lying Low', *Yorkshire Post and Leeds Intelligencer*, 10 November 1922, 8.

64 Alexander Scott MacCallum (1874–1928), Liberal and Coalition Liberal MP for Glasgow Bridgeton (1910–22).

65 'National Liberals Lying Low', *Yorkshire Post and Leeds Intelligencer*, 10 November 1922, 8.

66 'Remarkable election meeting Scene', *Belfast News-Letter*, 15 November 1922, 5.

Chapter 11

Final positions

In the last few days of the campaign, with an uneasy truce holding at the national level, and the *Daily Express* suggesting a Conservative majority of twenty-five, the leading politicians attempted to reinforce the positions of their respective camps with speeches in the constituencies.[1] The following list of speakers and their engagements in the last days of the election does suggest some patterns. Some of the main speakers such as Lloyd George and Walter Guinness had already been returned unopposed following the closure of nominations and could devote their time to supporting party colleagues in more difficult seats. Peers were also much in evidence in giving speeches for the same reason that they too did not face the prospect of losing their seats.

Friday 10 November
Lloyd George (Coalition Liberal) at Swansea and Haverfordwest
Marquess Salisbury (Conservative) at Newport
Sir Arthur Griffith Boscawen (Conservative) at Hull
Leopold Amery (Conservative) at Rugby
H. A. L. Fisher (Coalition Liberal) at Middleton (Lancashire)
Asquith (Liberal) at Paisley
Lord Derby (Conservative) at Accrington
J. H. Thomas (Labour) at Derby
Lord Birkenhead (Coalition Conservative) at Bedford
Walter Guinness (Conservative) at Darlington
Sir John Simon (Liberal) at Spenn Valley

Saturday 11 November

Bonar Law (Conservative) at Manchester and Sheffield
Baldwin (Conservative) at Newcastle
Lord Peel (Conservative) at Walsall
Lord Cave (Conservative) at Portsmouth
J. R. Clynes (Labour) at Oldham
Walter Guinness (Conservative) at Preston
Lloyd George (Coalition Liberal) on way to Criccieth speaking at Llanelly, Camarthen and Aberystwyth
Lord Birkenhead and Austen Chamberlain (Coalition Conservatives) at Birmingham
Asquith (Liberal) at Leicester
Sir Robert Horne (Coalition Conservative) at Glasgow
Churchill (Coalition Liberal) at Dundee
J. H. Thomas (Labour) at Manchester
Walter Runcimann (Liberal) at Gateshead
Lord Derby (Conservative) at Southport and Leigh

Monday 13 November

Bonar Law (Conservative) at Glasgow
Lord Peel (Conservative) at Brighton
Douglas Hogg (Conservative) at Reading
Lord Birkenhead (Coalition Conservative) at Ilkeston
Lloyd George (Coalition Liberal) at Denbigh and Flint
Asquith (Liberal) at Paisley
Lord Grey (Liberal) at Berwick
Churchill (Coalition Liberal) at Dundee
Duke of Devonshire (Conservative) at Dudley
Lord Long (Conservative) at Devizes
Lord Derby (Conservative) at Oldham

Tuesday 14 November

Lloyd George (Coalition Liberal) at Oldham, Bolton, Stockport, Bristol and five other locations
Lord Peel (Conservative) at Salisbury
Lord Londonderry (Conservative) at Hartlepool
Lord Long (Conservative) at Swindon
Lord Birkenhead (Coalition Conservative) at Southampton

Lord Grey (Liberal) at Berwick
J. H. Thomas (Labour) at Derby
J. R. Clynes (Labour) at Manchester
Bonar Law (Conservative) at Glasgow

For some of the Bonar Law camp it was a matter of being seen to support the parliamentary aspirations of the Coalition Liberals. For example, on 13 November at Dudley the Duke of Devonshire had made a speech praising the value of 'team work' and expressing great respect for 'the splendid part Mr. Lloyd George and his Government played in the war'.[2] The wider intended audience for the speech was evident from the fact that the fight at Dudley was a straight contest between the Conservatives and the Labour Party. Other signals were also being sent. For example, Lloyd George at Colwyn Bay, speaking in support of J. C. Davies, who was facing a three-cornered contest against a Conservative and an Asquithian Liberal, used the opportunity to attack the rival Liberal camp. He condemned those Liberals who might hand the Conservatives a large enough majority to give free rein to die-hardism.[3] He also played the anti-socialist card as he spoke at Pennygroes where the National Liberal candidate was involved in a straight fight with Labour. Calling on Conservative voters in particular, Lloyd George asked the electorate to deliver a defeat to Labour that would check their schemes which would inevitably damage national prosperity.[4]

The speech by Lord Birkenhead at Ilkeston on 13 November came in support of General J. E. B. Seeley, also facing a strong challenge from Labour, who were buoyed by the intervention of a Conservative candidate. Birkenhead's support of 'one of his oldest private and political friends' and call for Conservatives 'not to waste their votes' was capped with an appeal to the electorate not to potentially gift the seat to Labour.[5] Given Birkenhead's unpopularity, this perhaps rather ran counter to Seely's careful political fence-sitting up to this point as he attempted to attract votes from Liberals of both persuasions.

The following day, on 14 November, with just one day to go before polling, Lord Derby's speech to Lancashire Conservatives at Oldham (a two-member constituency which would elect a Conservative and a Coalition Liberal) was a final effort to get Lancashire Conservatives to support Coalition Liberals. He expressed great pride in the fact that 'there isn't a single National Liberal candidate being opposed by a Conservative candidate in the county of Lancashire'.[6]

Bonar Law used his final speech of the campaign to reiterate the four main themes which he suggested constituted the Conservative appeal to the nation:

1. National economy, with a view to the easing of the crushing burden of taxation.
2. A policy of non-interference with trade and commerce, giving an opportunity for an industrial revival.
3. The strengthening of the Entente with France, impaired by Lloyd Georgism.
4. The abandonment of wild-cat adventures at home and abroad.[7]

While the last two of these points expressed criticism of Lloyd George and his former regime, the first two were sufficiently general as to create grounds for co-operation with like-minded politicians in other parties after the election.

Lloyd George for his part, taking the final day to deliver nine speeches as he travelled from Lancashire to Bristol, reiterated the need for voters to elect progressive candidates who would rein in reaction on one side and keep socialism out on the other. This was further emphasised in a written appeal to voters in Scotland in which he expressed hopes that:

> 'I hope my friends in Scotland (both men and women) will come out to-morrow to vote for the candidates who are opposing Socialism ... I am looking forward to the return to the new Parliament of men of progressive ideals as a move against reaction on the one hand and revolutionary extremes on the other'.[8]

On the other side of the 'co-operation' fence, speaking that same day was Lord Beaverbrook in East Dorset who was doing his best to sabotage the election chances of Freddie Guest by publicly supporting the Unionist candidate the night before the election. Beaverbrook appeared at Poole to deliver his most emphatic attack on the National Liberals. Supporting the publisher and Conservative candidate Gordon Hall Caine, Beaverbrook argued: 'The Coalition Liberal was a very dangerous man at this moment. If he gets to Westminster ... a representation of 50 or 60, even 40 Members, he will hold the balance of power'.[9] His attempt to depersonalise the nature of his intervention against Guest by talking about 'The Coalition Liberal' probably went unappreciated by the former Coalition Liberal chief whip.

Notes

1 'Sure Triumph of Conservatives', *The Daily Express*, 14 November 1922, 1.

2 'No sensations', *Sheffield Daily Telegraph*, 14 November 1922. 7.

3 'Blood-Letting', *Sheffield Daily Telegraph*, 14 November 1922, 7.

4 'Blood-Letting', *Sheffield Daily Telegraph*, 14 November 1922, 7.

5 'Lord Birkenhead', *Nottingham Journal*, 14 November 1922, 14.

6 'National Liberals – Lord Derby Supports Co-operation', *Sheffield Daily Telegraph*, 14 November 1922, 7.

7 'General Election Polls Today', *Belfast News-Letter*, 15 November 1922, 5.

8 'Ex-premier's Tour Over', *Belfast News-Letter*, 15 November 1922, 5.

9 'A Dangerous Man', *Sheffield Daily Telegraph*, 15 November 1922, 5.

Chapter 12

The day of the election and the hours after

Lloyd George, accompanied by Megan Lloyd George, travelled to Bedford on the 9.25 a.m. to make a last-ditch speech for Frederick Kellaway,[1] who was facing a four-cornered fight in Bedford. Facing 3,000 voters, his speech betrayed a certain nervousness as he attacked the Independent Liberal candidate for splitting local Liberal forces.[2] Arriving back at St Pancras station at 1.25 p.m. he was whisked away by car to vote at Caxton Hall. This was part of what the *Daily Mirror* described as a 'busy day' for the ex-prime minister.[3]

The weather for election day in Scotland was particularly favourable, mild and 'almost windless', although the morning started out foggy in Glasgow and the day remained rather grey. Commentators considered that the lack of rain would lead to a good turnout amongst female voters.[4] Party activists made a final push for votes, in some cases using cars adorned with placards. In those areas where schools were being used as polling stations, throngs of children given the day off as a result added to the sense of excitement and occasion. Outside the polls women voluntary workers for the parties ticked off the electoral roll as voters arrived at the polling station. In some cases they minded children and the babies of women voters who preferred to leave them outside. Report after report for constituencies in Edinburgh and Glasgow emphasised the presence of women voters. For Edinburgh South a commentator for *The Scotsman* wrote: 'The women were in a great many instances accompanied by their family, and possibly never before have so many children been in the polling booths'.[5]

While comment was almost universally appreciative of women voters, in some cases commentators preferred to treat it as a matter for comedy. One London hack later wrote of his experiences on election day:

> 'How are you going to vote, Mrs. Brown?' I asked the family charwoman this morning. She answered, 'I don't know yet, sir: my husband hasn't made his mind up yet.' Whether many London women were content as she was to leave the decision to a husband, I do not pretend to know, but I have noticed to-day a large number of married couples entering the polling booths together. In fact, when I myself was voting I saw a young husband and wife rebuked by the returning officer because, after they had gone to adjoining desks, she filled up her paper and pushed it round the screen to her husband, loudly asking, 'Is this right?'[6]

In some constituencies the job of voting had been massively eased by the process of seat re-distribution and an increase in the number of polling stations. For example, at Saffron Walden the geographical area covered by the constituency had halved and there were eighty-five polling stations as opposed to nineteen in 1910.[7] In the more compact Southend constituency, by contrast, there were thirty-six polling stations. Of course, in very rural areas the distances that needed to be traversed by some voters remained considerable and in parts of rural Scotland there were suggestions that the unseasonal fine weather, and crofters' desire to make the most of it instead of taking half a day to get to and from the poll, had suppressed the vote.

In the Gorbals on the day of the election John Maclean, the Communist candidate, had the services of a band in fancy dress, while in Manchester (Platting) the campaign of J. R. Clynes, the Labour leader, was supported by an unofficial junior percussion band of children wearing sashes and armed with dustbin lids as cymbals.[8] Elsewhere in Glasgow a group of around 250 of the unemployed paraded in central areas with the banner '1914 on War Service; 1922 Starving'.[9] In Islington a group of children paraded with a banner saying 'Tax Wealth, Not Health'.[10] There was a carnivalesque element to proceedings in several other constituencies.

Cars were in evidence in many constituencies. Their number was surprisingly high with, for example, almost 200 being used at Colchester by the Conservatives in support of Sir Laming Worthington-Evans.[11] At Southend the Conservative candidate had one hundred cars at his disposal and the Liberals thirty. In the Buckrose constituency of the East Riding, the Conservatives deployed one car at each of the 120 rural polling stations, and around eighteen in each of the towns. The Asquith Liberal candidate meanwhile had just twenty-five: a differential which he later described as the principal cause of his defeat.[12] Unfortunately for Winston Churchill in Dundee, one of the cars being used to take Liberal voters to the polls knocked over and killed a black cat, which was taken as an ill omen of his fortunes.[13]

After the polls closed the first results began to come in just after 10 p.m. on 15 November as the Conservatives retained Wakefield, Wallasey and Bury. Soon after came news that Yarmouth, held since 1906 by veteran Conservative Sir Arthur Fell, had fallen to the Asquith Liberals. In these four seats special dispensation had been given for the polls to close at 8 p.m., hence they were first to issue returns.[14] Beaverbrook, at home with his family and a couple of guests, became nervous after hearing the result from Oxford, where the Liberal candidate had beaten the Conservative in a seat which they had held since 1880. Concerned at the result, and at the slow pace of the declarations, only slightly offset by the fact that it was clear that Coalition Liberal candidates were not doing well, he set off for the *Daily Express* offices where he found the staff 'gloomy and depressed' as the results were chalked up on blackboards.[15] In the boroughs Labour was performing much better than expected. As they put the first edition to bed for the morning's newsstands the headlines in the *Daily Express* reflected the mood: 'Heavy Conservative Losses'.[16] It was going to be a long night but it was clear which way the tide was flowing.

The same sense of foreboding was evident in Downing Street where Bonar Law sat with some of his closest political associates monitoring events. By 11 p.m. ten results had come in, including news that the Coalition Liberal seat of Barnsley had fallen to Labour. Bonar Law was deeply troubled at the prospect of his own defeat in Glasgow Central. The city with over half a million voters (301,586 male and 206,061 female), spread across fifteen seats, contested by forty candidates (ten Conservative, six National Liberal, ten Asquith Liberal, twelve Labour and two Communist) had seen some of the bitterest political fighting in the run up to the poll.[17] The election was to transform the political landscape of the city and, as Bonar Law waited on the national results, the performance of the Conservatives in Glasgow and across the country was less than encouraging. By 12 p.m. more than fifty results were in across the country and several features of the results were evident: a high turnout compared to 1918, a strong performance from Labour and a poor night for the Lloyd George Liberals, who had lost five seats in the early returns. The anti-socialist pact to shut Labour out of Westminster seats appeared to be performing poorly. It wasn't until 2 a.m. that the result in Glasgow Central came in: Bonar Law had retained his seat with a majority of 2,514 (a majority that had reduced by over 10,000 since 1918). Relieved and disappointed by his own result, Bonar Law went home to Onslow Gardens troubled by the possibility that the county results yet to come would not yield him a majority, even with the tacit support of the Coalition Liberals.

Bonar Law's mood was matched by that of Lloyd George, Birkenhead and some of the Conservative ex-ministers who had gathered at Sir Philip Sassoon's house in London to have dinner and wait for the results.[18] A ticker tape machine had been installed in Sassoon's dining room and as it beat out the results a sense of gloom filled the room. Early results suggested that the anti-socialists had not done enough to keep Labour away from breaking through in borough seats.

Across the country the public mood was more party-like. In London special election late-night/early-morning trains, buses and trams were laid on and posters made commuters and potential revellers aware of the routes and where they might see the results come through.[19] Trains would run from central locations until 2 a.m.[20] and trams and buses (from Charing Cross, Oxford Circus, Picadilly Circus and the Strand) every fifteen minutes until 2 a.m.[21] The underground would operate on the same basis.[22] At Trafalgar Square as many as 50,000 people watched as the election results came in. The crowds spilled out along the Strand, Picadilly and Regent Street where the results were projected onto screens as they were relayed by Marconi wireless. This was a real innovation, as broadcasting in the UK, bar some test broadcasts, had begun only the day before the election.[23] In London, news of victories and defeats around the country, relayed by wireless and telephone, were treated with cheers and boos. Newsreel cameramen for Pathé and at least one other company caught the atmosphere, with the crowd illuminated by searchlights occasionally picking out some of the women in the crowd, or the throwing of a streamer or handfuls of confetti in response to the latest news.[24] Street hawkers descended on the crowd to sell false noses and paper beards and other articles for celebration, such as sparklers and fireworks. As the fog slowly rose bonfires were lit in Trafalgar Square. Results no longer seemed to matter as the spontaneous public party took on a mood that correspondents later described as 'bedlam', 'pandemonium' and 'a beanfeast'.[25] Some of the larger hotels (Metropole), restaurants (Criterion and Trocadero) and clubs also found means to relay results to their diners, members and guests, and results were announced following the closure of the evening performances in nine theatres/picture houses, including the Hackney Empire and Leicester Palace.[26] With the results still coming in during the next day, some of the larger West End stores (Harrods, Barkers, Selfridges, Whiteley's)[27] used their public address systems to announce the continuing flow of results. Results were also available in other locations, including Fleet Street and Picadilly Circus.

In other parts of the country too, wireless or telephone was the means by which national election news was received and publicly relayed at local newspaper offices or at certain other business premises. In Leamington Spa the local newspaper took its results via telephone line from the Press Agency before projecting them onto a screen in Bedford Street.[28] Waiting for the first results, images of the different party leaders were projected onto the screen. Likewise, in Reading the *Reading Observer* received poll news via wireless and displayed it outside its offices.[29] In Chelmsford in Essex election news was broadcast from the windows of the Saracen's Head Hotel through a loudspeaker hooked up to a radio, and in Surrey two radio retailers used Marconi sets hooked up to loudspeakers to demonstrate their wares to the public in Reigate and Redhill.[30]

For those members of the middle class who had a wireless receiver, and were within 180 miles of one of the broadcast stations, it was possible to sit at home and listen as the results were broadcast from London, Manchester and Birmingham. Given the technology of the day, only one or two people at a time could listen to the results at home through a single earpiece.[31]

In Portsmouth a slightly different arrangement was used with results displayed on a screen at the top of the town hall steps. Results would be relayed to the town hall via one of the local newspaper offices by Post Office telegraph set up in the building. During breaks in the flow of results, images of the king, local candidates and local views would be projected to entertain the crowds.[32] Although a crowd of several thousand people had assembled to watch the results they were very quiet, certainly when compared to the scenes in London.

Notes

1 Frederick Kellaway (1870–1933), Liberal and later Coalition Liberal MP for Bedford (1910–22), Secretary for Overseas Trade (1920–21), Postmaster General (1921–22).

2 'Lloyd George at Bedford', *Gloucestershire Echo*, 15 November 1922, 6.

3 'Polling Scenes – Mr Lloyd George's Busy Day', *Daily Mirror*, 16 November 1922, 1.

4 'Incidents of the Polling', *The Scotsman*, 16 November 1922, 6.

5 'South Division', *The Scotsman*, 16 November 1922, 6.

6 'London Day by Day', *Sheffield Daily Telegraph*, 16 November 1922, 6.

7 'Polling Incidents', *Chelmsford Chronicle*, 17 November 1922, 8.

8 J. R. Clynes, *Memoirs 1869–1924* (London : Hutchinson & Co., 1937), 327–8.

9 'In Fancy Dress', *The Scotsman*, 16 November 1922, 6.

10 'A Change of Front', *Yorkshire Post*, 16 November 1922, 4.

11 'Polling Incidents', *Chelmsford Chronicle*, 17 November 1922, 8. Sir Laming Worthington-Evans (1868–1931), Conservative and Coalition Conservative MP for Colchester (1910–29) and Westminster St George's (1929–31), Minister of Blockade (1918), Minister of Pensions (1919–20), Minister without Portfolio (1920–21), Secretary of State for War (1921–22 and 1924–29), Postmaster General (1923–24).

12 'Mr Fenby (Buckrose)', 3 January 1923, MS Bonham Carter 682 f67.

13 'Heavy Poll at Dundee', *The Scotsman*, 16 November 1922, 6.

14 'London News', *The Scotsman*, 16 November 1922, 7.

15 Beaverbrook, *The Decline and Fall of Lloyd George*, 219.

16 'Heavy Conservative Losses', *The Daily Express*, 16 November 1922, 1.

17 'Scenes in Glasgow', *The Scotsman*, 16 November 1922, 6.

18 Beaverbrook, *The Decline and Fall of Lloyd George*, 220.

19 'Election night poster', 15 November 1922, Action Department, Underground Electric Railway Company Ltd, Item 1983/4/1385, London Transport Museum.

20 'Election night poster', Action Department, Underground Electric Railway Company Ltd, Item 1983/4/8203, London Transport Museum.

21 'Election night poster', Action Department, Underground Electric Railway Company Ltd, Item 2005/7063 part 123, London Transport Museum.

22 'Election night poster', Action Department, Underground Electric Railway Company Ltd, Item 2005/7063 part 122, London Transport Museum.

23 'Broadcasting', *Sheffield Daily Telegraph*, 16 November 1922, 6.

24 ‘Our London Letter’, *Derby Daily Telegraph*, 17 November 1922, 6.

25 ‘Our London Letter’, *Derby Daily Telegraph*, 17 November 1922, 6.

26 ‘How to Learn results’, *Pall Mall Gazette*, 14 November 1922, 3.

27 ‘Election night poster’, Action Department, Underground Electric Railway Company Ltd, Item 2005/7063 part 133, London Transport Museum.

28 ‘Receiving Election Results’, *Leamington Spa Courier*, 17 November 1922, 4.

29 ‘Reading and the General Election’, *Reading Observer*, 17 November 1922, 1.

30 ‘Polling Incidents’, *Chelmsford Chronicle*, 17 November 1922, 8. ‘Listening in at Reigate’, *Surrey Mirror*, 17 November 1922, 5.

31 ‘Election Results at Home by Wireless’, *Sheffield Daily Telegraph*, 17 November 1922, 4.

32 ‘The Results on the Screen’, *Hampshire Telegraph*, 17 November 1922, 11.

Chapter 13

Results

Following the election it took the best part of another day for the electoral patterns to become clear, and those patterns would cast a long shadow over the interwar period. While Labour had done very well in the boroughs, in the counties they had performed much worse. Bonar Law's Conservatives would have a substantial majority and the hopes of the Lloyd George Liberals to hold the balance of power had been dashed. The *Daily Express* of 17 November carried the headline: 'Dominating Conservative Majority'.[1] In *The Decline and Fall of Lloyd George*, Lord Beaverbrook relates that Lloyd George and his circle were full of open fury against him. They depicted him as a man who had not sought power through the endorsement of the electorate: instead, he sought to be the power behind the throne exercising a hidden influence upon events.[2]

Lloyd George's strategy had been defeated by the shift of the electorate towards the Conservatives and Labour, and the breakdown of some local pacts had cost them dear in particular seats. As Morgan has written: 'In the circumstances, to hold on to over fifty seats was a meritorious achievement. It was at least a useful bargaining counter for Lloyd George'.[3] The key thing is that many of them had been returned as a result of their personal standing within their constituencies rather than as a result of enthusiasm for Lloyd George's brand of Liberalism, and they would be useful elements in the process of Liberal reunion in 1923 rather than as a useful bargaining counter in terms of the formation of the government in 1922. The weakness of the Coalition Liberal cause was further underlined by the fact that so many Liberal ex-ministers had fallen at the election. 'Churchill, Guest, Montagu, Greenwood and Kellaway had all fallen'.[4] At least, however, the Coalition Liberal ranks had been swelled by rising Liberal stars such as

Archibald Sinclair and Geoffrey Shakespeare and the victories included 'five of the ten seats lost in by-elections'.[5] With the numbers of Lloyd George and the Asquith Liberals evenly balanced, the path towards eventual Liberal reunification in 1923 was eased considerably.

It is a truism that every general election breaks down into over 600 separate constituency contests. In the circumstances of 1922 that was especially true with the undeclared and partial truce between the Conservatives and Coalition Liberals which saw 'local arrangements' in place in many areas. Partial Liberal reunification in Manchester, Leeds and Sunderland with candidates standing without particular affiliation to either Lloyd George or Asquith added a further layer of complication. The Coalition Liberal losses, and victories, in 1922 hid many quirks which have skewed attempts at statistical analysis. Indeed, as much as it is desirable from a psephological perspective to organise and codify the data, and to make the 1922 General Election accessible and comparable in statistical terms to other elections, the political realities make this all but impossible. At every turn there are issues as regards how to interpret the data in an election in which many candidates, by one means or another, had a problem with narrow definition of their loyalties.

Quirks and anomalies were one of the hallmarks of an election in which at least six children under the age of thirteen voted after having been included on the electoral roll, while trouble was also experienced with absentee ballots for those on military service, despite considerable efforts in 1920 and 1921 to remedy a problem that had dogged the 1918 election.[6] In the case of North East Derbyshire the unsuccessful Liberal Candidate (he had lost to the Labour candidate by five votes) launched a petition against the outcome of the election when two uncounted ballot papers were discovered on the return of the ballot boxes to County Hall in Derby.[7] In the subsequent recount the majority of his Labour opponent was increased to fifteen.

The problem of party labels is the major complicating factor in calculations about the party performances of 1922. On 1 November, as the closure of nominations approached, local Conservative grandee Maynard Colchester Weymss in the Forest of Dean had expressed the wonderment of many in 1922: 'how many candidates there will be, & how they will be labelled'.[8] *The Times* newspaper wrestled with the problem of party labels following the closure of nominations. Using information supplied by the parties centrally, then cross-referenced with local constituency associations, on 6 November *The Times* arrived at the figures in Table 13.1 for the

Table 13.1: 1922 General Election: numbers of prospective parliamentary candidates

Party	Numbers
Conservative	444
Labour and Cooperative	412
Liberal	339
National Liberal	138

numbers of prospective parliamentary candidates being put forward by the parties.

The Lloyd George and Asquith Liberals being put forward in those places where partial liberal reunification had taken place were classified as 'Liberal'.[9] Likewise nine of the ten members of the National Democratic Party (Labour MPs who supported Lloyd George during the war and took the coupon in 1918), such as Clement Edwards in East Ham South, were classed as National Liberals.

The analysis by *The Times* suggested that, at least in part, pacts between the parties had limited the number of three-cornered contests in which the centre-right parties might fight against each other to the benefit of Labour. In 57 out of 615 seats there was no contest, with only one candidate standing, such as David Lloyd George in Caernarvon. In a further 373 seats there was a straight fight between two candidates, with just 242 seats involving multi-party battles. In twenty-six constituencies (less than five per cent of the whole) there were four-cornered contests, in East Ham North there were five, and five also in the two-member constituencies of Blackburn, Bolton and Oldham. In Sunderland, Southampton and Dundee (also two-member constituencies) there were six candidates.

To this quantitative data, in trying to drill further down, there can be added some impressions gained by the Asquith Liberals in late 1922 and early 1923 as they tried to come to terms with the results and the emerging postwar political landscape. The Asquith Liberals, perhaps more than any other party, tried to understand the nature of the 1922 election. They took a keen interest in what might be described as the state of the Liberal vote in particular constituencies. For example, Sir William Edge had been re-elected for the Lloyd George Liberals in the two-member constituency of Bolton in 1922 with 31,015 votes, behind the Conservative with 37,491. The two Labour candidates came third and fourth, and the Asquith Liberal a distant fifth with 18,534. The importance of the local party pact was evidenced in a later report that suggested that only around 5,000 of Edge's votes came from voters who could be considered 'Liberal'.[10] Likewise in the Aberavon constituency, won by Ramsay MacDonald from the National Liberals, local analysis suggested that of the 34,000 registered voters, only 12,000 could be considered Liberal, with a further 7,000 likely Conservative, giving a Labour maximum of 14,000.[11] Without an anti-socialist coalition Aberavon was effectively going to be henceforth a very safe Labour seat.

For all parties, analysing the results was complicated by the diversity of labels for candidates. Add in the operation of the coupon in 1918, and one or two other quirks, and a precise accounting of the outcome of the general election was, and remains, all but impossible. For example, Halifax had been captured by the Coalition Liberals in 1918 by John Whitley, who had first been elected as a Liberal in 1906. In 1921 he was elected as speaker of the House, becoming nominally neutral/independent. In 1922 his seat went uncontested in line with the convention that the other parties did not contest the speaker's constituency. His seat therefore appears as a theoretical loss to the Lloyd George Liberals from 1918 to 1922 when, in fact, it was retained by the same MP who had won it for them at the Coupon Election.[12] This issue of party label in the accountancy of party performance affected a number of other constituencies. For example, in Eye (Suffolk) Alexander Lyle-Samuel had won the seat as a Coalition Liberal in 1918 and had won it again in 1922, although this time as an Asquith Liberal, as he had broken with the Lloyd George government in 1921.[13] In the process he defeated by 3,531 votes his only opponent, Gerald Howard, the Lloyd George Liberal candidate who enjoyed at least the passive support of the local Conservative Association. Thus, while the seat did not change hands in terms of the sitting member it did equate to a loss to the Coalition Liberals and a victory for the Asquith Liberals.

The haphazard way in which the coupon had been applied in 1918 was, perhaps, the largest single factor adding to complications as to the arithmetic of the Coalition Liberal performance. For example, with the Mossley constituency in Lancashire, the seat had been won in 1918 by Austin Hopkinson, an independent candidate who nevertheless took the Coalition Liberal whip.[14] He was one of seven or eight MPs elected without the coupon in 1918 who took the government whip on entering the House of Commons. Hopkinson won the seat again in 1922 as an independent, so that Mossley is frequently counted as a Coalition Liberal loss.

Another example, of the coupon potentially skewing calculations of seat losses in 1922 occurred with the Sudbury constituency in Suffolk. In 1918 the seat was won by tenant farmer Stephen Howard as a Liberal, despite the fact that the coupon went to the Unionist candidate Richard Proby.[15] On election Howard, like Hopkinson, agreed to take the government whip. In 1922 Howard again contested the constituency, this time as an avowed Lloyd George Liberal. He came second to the Unionist candidate as the Liberal vote was split by the Asquithian Liberal candidate who came third. Sudbury was an effective loss for the Lloyd George Liberals, although on any analysis of the transfer of seats between 1918 and 1922 it might count as a Unionist gain from Liberal.

Liberal reunification in some areas adds a further level of complication. The Coalition Liberal was defeated by the Labour candidate in Leeds South, and in Leeds North and Central the Conservatives gained the seat from sitting Coalition Liberals. Only in Leeds West did John Murray, who had been elected as Coalition Liberal in 1918, retain his seat. Three Leeds seats won in 1918 by the Coalition Liberals (two with the same candidate) fell to either Conservatives or Labour in 1922: the accountancy of the general election was complicated by the fact that in 1922 a reunified local party supported each 'Liberal' prospective parliamentary candidate.

To add to the confusion, the politics of some candidates makes it almost impossible to discern their true party affiliations. In 1922 Barnet Kenyon was returned unopposed for the Chesterfield Division. Pit worker, union official and Primitive Methodist preacher, in 1913 he had been selected by the Derbyshire miners to fight the constituency after the death of the sitting Labour member. Kenyon also managed to secure the nomination of the local Liberals and he easily beat the Conservative into second place. In the Coupon Election he was variously listed as the Labour candidate and as the Coalition Liberal candidate in receipt of the coupon. His nomination was also endorsed by some local Conservatives. He was returned unopposed even though he also appeared to support the Asquith Liberal cause elsewhere in Derbyshire. In 1922 he was again returned unopposed with a variety of party labels being applied to his success. The *Sheffield Telegraph*, conservative and working class, listed him amongst the Coalition Liberal successes.[16] In reality Kenyon was a one-man party pact between the major parties.

Likewise in Caernarvonshire Robert Jones's stunning win for Labour over the Coalition Liberal candidate Charles Breese by 1,609 votes was not perhaps the victory for the Labour movement that it appeared. Most historians see it as evidence of Labour breaking through in north-west Wales, to complement its existing strength in South Wales, whereas Emyr Price's examination of Jones's election in 1922, and subsequent short-lived parliamentary career, calls into question whether his election 'constituted to any marked extent, a sharp disjuncture with traditional politics' in the region.[17] His moderation on most matters led some to wonder whether Jones's sympathies lay more with Asquith than with Clynes and MacDonald.

Local complexities, the circumstances of the 1922 election and the granting of the coupon in 1918, together with the changing allegiances of some candidates, provides considerable qualification to any attempt to reach categorical statistical understandings of the 1922 General Election. In spite of this, however, their representation fell by over half, from 122 to around 57. Had it not been for the absence of Tory opposition in English and Scottish constituencies, this representation might have been cut by at least two-thirds.[18] In Scotland, the truce between the parties had been highly effective. As Chris Cook notes, only in two constituencies, Perth and Glasgow Cathcart, had the pact between Conservatives and Coalition Liberals broken down.[19] In some places Lloyd George Liberals made progress against the rising tide of socialism. At Kirkaldy Burghs, a traditional Liberal seat, captured by Labour in 1921 at a by-election with a majority of 1,473, former soldier Sir Robert Hutchinson captured the seat for the National Liberals from the incumbent socialist with a majority of 683. Hutchinson's appeal to the electors was based very firmly on the idea of coalition against 'the wild theories expressed in the Labour manifesto'.[20]

In England, beyond Lord Derby's fiefdom of Lancashire Conservatism, the breakdown of relations with the Conservatives brought notable losses of senior Coalition Liberals. For example, the defeat of Major J. E. B. Seely in Ilkeston was 'fully expected' with the intervention of a Conservative candidate.[21] The response to his defeat did at least suggest continuing strong support for co-operation in the name of anti-socialism, with the *Derby Daily Telegraph* launching an extraordinary attack on the actions of Marshall Freeman in letting his name go forward, and towards Bonar Law for endorsing him.[22] Defeated by 1,084 votes, the 5,841 votes that went to Freeman had been, in the opinion of the *Derby Daily Telegraph*, pivotal in gifting the seat to the socialists. The newspaper's attack was expressed in personal and emotional terms: 'We experience no little difficulty in coming to this conclusion – that there is more joy in Birmingham over the defeat of a Coalition Liberal than regret at the triumph of an out and out advocate of Labour policy'.[23] The imperative for the newspaper did appear, however, to be anti-socialism, rather than out-and-out support for co-operation. Despite earlier condemnation of the emergence of a Conservative candidate in neighbouring South Derbyshire, the same newspaper was more than ready after the poll to accept the victory of Henry Lorimer,[24] who beat Samuel Truman the Labour candidate into second place with a majority of 4,463.

Beyond the general lines of Labour progress, Conservative revival and Liberal stasis (artificially supported by local pacts), one other noteworthy lesson to emerge from the election was in relation to the women's vote, which the Coalition Liberals had set great store by. While the votes cast by women remained a subject of conjecture, the failure of women candidates to get elected in 1922 perhaps cast a long shadow over the hopes for more balanced gender representation in the House of Commons in the interwar period. Of the twenty-six women candidates to stand, only two were returned: Nancy Astor for the Conservatives with a majority of 3,903 and Margaret Winteringham for the Liberals with a majority of 83, down on her 1920 by-election majority of 791.[25] Of the remaining candidates, many fighting in seats considered hopeless by the parties that had put them forward, only three were denied by slim majorities numbering in the hundreds. The other twenty-one were defeated by thousands of votes. The electorate appeared lukewarm to the idea of women members of parliament, and the issue of the women's vote, which could be captured en-masse with the right policies, continued to remain something of an elusive enigma to the political parties. As Maynard Colchester Weymss noted:

> One curious feature of the Election is that it is the first General Election in which women have had the vote, great doubt was felt as to how they would vote, and I am inclined to think that they now they actually did vote, & will remain an enigma; but perhaps it is a still more curious feature that, though there were nearly 50 women candidates, all of them have been rejected except two, & both those two were [already] members of the House of Commons where they had both made their mark and they had succeeded in gaining the confidence & esteem of their constituents.[26]

Notes

1 'Dominating Conservative Majority', *The Daily Express*, 17 November 1922, 1.

2 Beaverbrook, *The Decline and Fall of Lloyd George*, 224.

3 Morgan, *Consensus and Disunity*, 358.

4 Morgan, 'Lloyd George's Stage Army', 250.

5 Morgan, 'Lloyd George's Stage Army', 250.

6 'The Child Voters', *Yorkshire Evening Post*, 16 November 1922, 6. Home Office Correspondence on the 1922 General Election in TNA: H045/11083.

7 NE Derbyshire Election Petition, TNA: LCO2/2576.

8 Maynard Colchester Weymss to the King of Siam, 1 November 1922, Gloucester Archives D37/1/445.

9 'Nominations Analysed', *The Times*, 6 November 1922, 14.

10 'Mr Holt (Bolton)', 28 September 1923, MS Bonham Carter 682 f77.

11 'Mr Watts (Aberavon)', 12 October 1923, MS Bonham Carter 682 f78.

12 John Whitley (1866–1935), Liberal MP (1900–18), Coalition Liberal (1918–21), Independent (1921–28) for Halifax.

13 Alexander Lyle-Samuel (1883–1942) Coalition Liberal (1918–circa 1921) and Liberal MP for Eye (1921–23).

14 Austin Hopkinson (1879–1962), Liberal MP for Prestwich (1918), Independent MP for Mossley (1918–29, 1931–45).

15 Stephen Howard (1867–1934), Liberal MP for Sudbury (1918–22).

16 'The Walk-Over', *Sheffield Daily Telegraph*, 6 November 1922, 7.

17 Emyr Price, 'Labour's "Breakthrough" in Caernarfon County in 1922: The Election of R T Jones to Westminster', *Caernarvonshire Historical Transactions* 64 (2003): 94–119.

18 Morgan, 'Lloyd George's Stage Army', 250.

19 Cook, *The Age of Alignment*, 17.

20 'Kirkcaldy's Choice', *The Scotsman*, 3 November 1922, 7.

21 'Other Derbyshire Seats', *Sheffield Independent*, 17 November 1922, 4.

22 'Notes on Current Events', *Derby Daily Telegraph*, 28 November 1922, 2.

23 'Notes on Current Events', *Derby Daily Telegraph*, 28 November 1922, 2.

24 Henry Lorimer (1879–1933), Conservative MP for South Derbyshire (1922–24).

25 'How Women have Fared', *Yorkshire Evening Post*, 16 November 1922, 10.

26 Maynard Colchester Weymss to the King of Siam, 15 November 1922, Gloucester Archives D37/1/447. The two women returned in 1922 had been elected in by-elections, Nancy Astor (Plymouth Sutton, Conservative, 1919) and Margaret Wintringham (Louth, Liberal, 1921).

Chapter 14

Repercussions of the 1922 General Election

The outcomes of the 1922 General Election were profound for all concerned. For the Conservative Party the election proved for the first time since 1900 that it could win an election in its own right. At the constituency level there was also rejoicing. For example, at Maldon in Essex, Edward Ruggles-Brise (1882–1942), the victorious Conservative candidate, was deluged with mail from across the constituency and beyond (56 telegrams and 124 letters from Conservative supporters, fellow members of the landed gentry and commercial enterprises eager for his continued custom).[1] For many Conservatives the outcome of the 1922 General Election represented an unexpected victory, and a remarkable avoidance of several potentially disastrous outcomes. Despite the rupture at the Carlton Club meeting, with its rejection of most of the leadership of the Conservative Party, the absence of party controversy, the willingness of Bonar Law to accept 'local arrangements', and the threat from Labour largely preserved harmony in the constituencies. As Stuart Ball has commented: 'Above all, disunity was not carried into the constituencies. There was no purge of MPs and almost no competing candidatures, and the fragmentation of the local organisation and of the Conservative vote was avoided'.[2] Without the leading lights of the Conservative Party, Bonar Law's 'Second XI' proved capable in the months following in an unspectacular and quiet way – exactly in line with the promises of the Conservative Party in the lead up to polling day.

The Labour Party could also claim victory in 1922. In some ways, Labour's triumph was even more significant than that of the Conservatives. It is perhaps the post-election euphoria at Labour's performance, and the eclipse of the Liberals, that limited the impact on later accounts of any concerns about the operation of unofficial Conservative/Coalition Liberal Pacts in many constituencies. Clynes, the Labour leader in 1922, makes no mention of them in his memoirs, but he is fulsome in his expression of joy at Labour's performance in the election.[3] Labour's breakthrough in the urban, industrial conurbations, with 142 seats secured, meant that the party became the official opposition in the House of Commons. The significance of the performance was evident at the time with one Scottish newspaper commenting: 'Taken all over the 1922 election is a triumph for Labour rather than for the Conservative party'.[4] Labour's breakthrough in 1922 transformed the parliamentary party in ways which enhanced its ability to appeal to the electorate in future elections. As David Marquand has noted:

> The new parliamentary Labour Party ... was a very different body from the old one. In 1918, 48 Labour MPs had been sponsored by trade unions, and only three by the ILP. Now about 100 members belonged to the ILP, while 32 had actually been sponsored by it, as against 85 who had been sponsored by trade unions. The change in class background was equally significant. In 1918, no Labour MPs had been to public schools, and only one to a university. Now there were 21 university graduates, and 9 public-school men ... In the country, the Labour Party was still an overwhelmingly working-class organization. In Parliament, it could present itself for the first time as the movement of opinion rather than of class.[5]

As Alan Ball has demonstrated, the impact of the 1922 General Election on the parliamentary Labour Party, including reforms designed to enhance the authority of the newly introduced post of chairman and leader, made it more electable, capable, and gave it greater independence from the rest of the party.[6] Just over a year later, following the 1923 General Election, the Labour Party under Ramsay MacDonald, who had gained his seat at Aberavon in 1922 from the sitting Coalition Liberal, would form a first minority administration, supplanting the Liberals as the second party in the two-party system.

The outcome of the 1922 election was not, however, uniformly positive in the long term for Labour as some of the very detailed local studies of the development of the Labour Party in this period have revealed.[7] As Clare Griffiths has noted, Labour had done well in urban areas but throughout the interwar period the party would struggle to make progress in winning over the rural working classes.[8] In addition, as Declan McHugh has demonstrated with regard to Manchester, support of the urban working classes would continue to be dependent on considerations of whether a vote for the Labour Party might result in improvements to their material conditions – engagement with the wider political goals of the party was limited.[9] Formidable obstacles would remain to the consolidation of Labour's hold on the industrial cities, as Sam Davies has demonstrated with his study of Liverpool.[10] Overall, though, the 1922 General Election gave Labour a sense of momentum and a sense that power was within their grasp.

What was good for the Labour and Conservative Parties was inevitably bad for Liberals of both persuasions. As David Dutton has written:

> In the event, neither Liberal faction had much cause for satisfaction. The Independent Liberals gained 43 seats, with a final total of 54 … But 14 seats were lost, 9 of them to Labour, and their showing in mining seats, where they had done well before 1914, was especially disappointing … The performance of the Lloyd Georgeites was, if anything, even worse.[11]

The level of Conservative success at the constituency level negated Lloyd George's strategy of trying to hold power with around seventy seats. In the event, the Coalition Liberals had fallen short of that level by seventeen seats, but even if they had reached that target, the Bonar Law administration would still have had a useful working majority. The Asquith Liberals had taken third place in the party stakes, but third place in a two-party system meant that both Liberal parties faced an existential threat underpinned by ongoing realignment of British party politics, a changing socio-economic electoral base, and further declines at the constituency level in terms of finances and activists. As Gavin Freeman has noted in respect of the decline of the Liberal Party in Leicestershire, with a divided party coming third and fourth in the general election the Liberals could not sit back and allow the natural swing of the pendulum to put them back into office at some point in the future.[12]

Amalgamation of the two wings of British Liberalism represented the only possible response to the threat. Reunion would follow within the year, impelled by the determination of Stanley Baldwin, who would replace the dying Bonar Law in May 1923, to call an election to introduce protectionist measures to safeguard British industries. The old Liberal rallying call of

'Free Trade' formed a convenient rationale for the party reunion that most within it regarded as a necessity. In that reunion the brand of National or Coalition Liberalism would be abandoned in favour of the older brand of Liberal Party controlled by Asquith, and in places like south-west Britain the party would experience something of a revival, as Gary Tregidga has charted.[13] Likewise, in the 1923 General Election the final fires of discord between Baldwin and the former coalitionist Conservatives would be extinguished by the cry of tariff reform and the reunion of the Liberals.[14]

Notes

1 Edward Ruggles-Brise papers, Essex Record Office, A5909 Box 22.

2 Stuart Ball, *The Conservative Party and British Politics 1902–1951* (New York: Routledge, 2013), 70.

3 Clynes, *Memoirs 1869–1924*, 327–30.

4 'The Election Results', *The Arbroath Herald*, 17 November 1922, 4.

5 Marquand, *Ramsay MacDonald*, 283.

6 See Alan R. Ball, *British Political Parties: The Emergence of a Modern Party System* (London: Palgrave, 1987), 108ff.

7 See for example, John Holford, *Reshaping Labour: Organization, Work and Politics in Edinburgh in the Great War and After* (New York: Croom Helm, 1988); Ian McLean, *The Legend of Red Clydeside* (Edinburgh: John Donald, 1983); Matthew Worley, *Labour's Grass Roots: Essays on the Activities of Local Labour Parties and Members, 1918–45* (London: Ashgate, 2005).

8 Clare Griffiths, *Labour and the Countryside: The Politics of Rural Britain, 1918–39* (Oxford: Oxford University Press, 2007).

9 Declan McHugh, *Labour in the City: The Development of the Labour Party in Manchester, 1918–31* (Manchester: Manchester University Press, 2006).

10 S. Davies, *Liverpool Labour: Social and Political Influences on the Development of the Labour Party, 1900–1939* (Keele: Keele University Press, 1996).

11 David Dutton, *A History of the Liberal Party Since 1900*, 2nd edition (Basingstoke: Palgrave, 2013), 83.

12 Gavin J. Freeman, 'The Decline of the Liberal Party in the Heart of England: The Liberals in Leicestershire, 1914–24', *Historical Research* 89, no. 3 (2016): 531–49 (543).

13 Gary Tregidga, *The Liberal Party in South-West Britain Since 1918: Political Decline, Dormancy and Rebirth* (Exeter: University of Exeter Press, 2000).

14 Chamberlain to Baldwin, 14 November 1923, Austen Chamberlain papers, Cadbury Research Library, AC35/3/3.

Conclusion

The 1922 General Election was in some senses the first 'modern' British election in which the majority of the adult population of the United Kingdom had the chance to democratically decide their parliamentary representation (constituency-based, first past the post) on a single day and in an event that felt national as opposed to narrowly local. The vast majority of those elected would come from the parties that would dominate British politics for the next century, with the Labour Party emerging as a potential party of government. The Conservative Party meanwhile would win its first general election since 1900 and would go on to dominate British politics during the mid to late twentieth century. It was part of what David Thackeray sees as a cultural transformation, by which the Conservative Party adapted itself to the changed, and changing, nature of early twentieth-century Britain.[1] The divided forces of British Liberalism were reduced to a disappointed third force, and the 1922 election underlined the fact that elections were an expensive business, with most candidates requiring financial support.[2] In a postwar age in which the aristocracy, and well-to-do supporters, were engaged in financial retrenchment the cost of doing business cast a long shadow over the forces of British Liberalism.

As much as it marked a beginning, the 1922 General Election also marked the beginning of the end of the politics of the pre-democratic age. The ramifications of the 1918 Representation of the People Act, and the wider repercussions of the First World War, had created a new electorate with a new set of concerns, calling for new approaches to politics and perhaps new political parties. Lloyd George firmly believed that anti-socialism versus socialism would be the new axis upon which British politics would turn and, in a sense, the Coalition Liberal Party was a milestone on the road to a new party in which Conservatism and Liberalism would be fused into a new progressive party. Lloyd George was obsessed with the threat from radical Labour, and initially took for granted the willingness of the rank and file of the Conservative Party to fall into line behind their party leadership and acquiesce in the emergence of a new party. Meanwhile, as Neal McCrillis has observed, the Conservative Party in its structures and culture was already well advanced in the process of adapting itself to the postwar age.[3]

Many Coalition Liberals and a good number of Conservatives genuinely believed in the idea of a progressive, anti-socialist alliance as a means to extend the patriotic co-operation that had secured victory in the First World War. That continuing spirit lay at the heart of the maintenance of local arrangements at the time of the 1922 General Election. Lloyd George's adherents were not simply careerists clinging to Lloyd George's coat tails and many Conservatives saw no good reason to overthrow good candidates in the aftermath of a war of shared national sacrifice, and pooled resources, for the sake of the national interest.

That the Coalition Liberals ultimately emerged from the 1922 election with over fifty members of parliament was a remarkable achievement, even if it did not hand Lloyd George the role of king-maker to the Bonar Law government. Whether the Coalition Liberals in 1922 would have done as well without the existence of local party pacts with the Conservative Party is open to question. Without those pacts the Coalition Liberal Party would have returned fewer members, but that was probably also true of the Conservative Party, and also true of the Asquith Liberals. As Michael Kinnear identified in the 1970s, in 1922 'over 200 Liberal and Conservative candidates ran under the aegis of two or more parties' including 'prefixless Liberals', 'Constitutionalists', 'Conservatives with Liberal support' and 'Liberals with Conservative support'.[4] In the circumstances of 1922, and the strong possibilities of some form of renewed coalition, some of these labels and local arrangements were vital to preventing a wider Labour breakthrough, but they also amounted to a hedging of bets by some candidates. In 1922 many had no wish to alienate sections of the electorate that might be persuaded to vote for them, and they had no wish to potentially exclude themselves from a role in whatever government might emerge from the election. So widespread were the local arrangements, and so loose were the party labels, that it really is difficult to think, except in the very broadest terms, of the 1922 contest as constituting a truly general election, carried out by truly national parties with centrally directed campaigns. Resolving the political landscape from the confusing mass of local arrangements and flag of convenience labels for many candidates took time after the election as members of parliament declared their allegiances by accepting party whips.

To some extent historians have failed to resolve the complexities of the election and that has fed through into historical understandings of the election. As the author of one work commented: 'The election results, devastating for the Liberals, speak for themselves. The Liberals, whether Asquithians or supporters of Lloyd George were reassured'.[5] While the two statements sit seemingly in opposition to each other, they were also largely true. Scovell and others were pleased at the Coalition Liberal returns, but in the longer term the holding action of 1922 failed to deliver Lloyd George the balance of power, and appeared in retrospect to be a key milestone on the road to Liberal irrelevance.

A seemingly confused election has resulted in a somewhat confused historiography, but we can go beyond the surface of explanations that the 1922 General Election, and with it the cause of Coalition Liberalism, was 'a curious affair'.[6] We can see that Lloyd George was much more than 'the ghost at the feast' after the Carlton Club meeting.[7] He was playing a high stakes game that he expected to win with the Coalition Liberal Party being part of his collateral. But so too was Bonar Law and his strategy included a greater number of options, including potentially a deal with the Asquithians. Ultimately Bonar Law played the game more effectively and his surprise victory robbed Lloyd George of the dramatic re-entrance at the head of his stage army under some new 'arrangement between the parties' that he so desperately craved. That surprise victory was testament to the vigour and strength of the Conservative Party beyond the parliamentary party, which meant that ultimately Conservatives considered that they no longer needed the man who won the war to win an election.

And what then of the Labour Party? While historians of the Conservative Party have emphasised the effectiveness of the Tory machine in the 1922 election victory, the strength of the Labour organisation under Arthur Henderson had been fully demonstrated during the campaign. Labour had run a tight, disciplined campaign in which candidates had been well supported at the local and national levels. Energised by the general election the Labour Party would continue to build its strength at the constituency level, and by the time of the party conference in 1923 only 6 of the 603 constituencies in England, Scotland and Wales did not have a local constituency Labour Party organisation. Women also continued to rally to Labour's cause with 120,000 women members of 1,031 women's organisations allied to local parties across the United Kingdom.[8] Meanwhile five full-time propagandists toured the country to rally support at the local level.[9] Labour's success in the 1923 general election campaign little more than one year later would allow Ramsay MacDonald to form a first Labour government.

Notes

1 David Thackeray, *Conservatism for the Democratic Age: Conservative Cultures and the Challenge of Mass Politics in Early Twentieth Century England* (Manchester: Manchester University Press, 2013).

2 See financial support for candidates in the 1922 General Election campaign listing subventions to each Liberal Party parliamentary candidate, MS Asquith 142.

3 Neal R. McCrillis, *The British Conservative Party in the Age of Universal Suffrage: Popular Conservatism, 1918–1929* (Columbus: Ohio State University Press, 1998).

4 Kinnear, *The Fall of Lloyd George*, 243.

5 Rosemary Rees, *Britain, 1890–1939* (London: Heinemann, 2003), 121.

6 Powell, *British Politics, 1910–35*, 118.

7 Powell, *British Politics, 1910–35*, 119.

8 Report of the 23rd Annual Conference, 45, Labour Party Archive, People's History Museum.

9 Report of the 23rd Annual Conference, 47, Labour Party Archive, People's History Museum.

Afterword: considerations for British politics

Long-term changes, such as the decline of particular sectors of the economy, or changing demographics within a society, can be energised by short-term factors (war, pandemics, etc.) to produce dramatic changes in the outlook and behaviour of electorates. Political parties, given traditional party-political processes, broad-church structures and historic identities, will almost inevitably struggle to respond to rapid and profound political shifts caused by socio-economic changes energised by short-term factors. In 1922 it was easier for the Conservative and Coalition Liberal Parties to base their electoral appeal on what they were not, or what they were against (socialism and militant labourism) rather than what they stood for except in the most general terms (peace in Europe, the League of Nations, Empire, moderation in spending, limited social provision). The Conservative Party, in particular, ran its campaign explicitly on the fact that it was 'not Lloyd George' because traditional policies such as Tariff Reform and Ireland appeared problematic or simply no longer relevant. This sense of the Conservatives and Liberals trying to craft new identities for themselves would continue during the interwar period but in 1922, 'Tranquillity and Peace' and 'Not Lloyd George' were something of a hostage to fortune, given the perceived likely outcome of the 1922 General Election and the strategic decision to leave the door open to 'a close working relationship' with the Lloyd Georgeites. The attempt to manage the election through maintaining, where possible, local pacts for the Conservatives to co-opt Lloyd George Liberals into the role of the new

Liberal Unionists, ran counter to what broad sections of the new British electorate actually wanted in 1922.

The Conservatives and Lloyd George Liberals, in thinking that a coalition was the most likely outcome of the 1922 General Election, not only 'misread the room', but also attempted to mislead its occupants with local arrangements and private promises of support by candidates that amounted to an unspoken pact of sorts between the parties at the national level. The moral of this story appeared to be that second guessing an electorate in the midst of a rapid political shift is exceptionally difficult.

However, in the twenty-first century party pacts remain on the table as a means of electoral management with the Electoral Commission having formally published advice on their nature and management.[1] In the General Election of 2019 the Conservative Party flirted with an electoral pact with the Brexit Party and, while it was rejected, the Brexit Party only stood in opposition-held seats. This helped to gift the Conservatives a majority of over seventy seats. While there is suspicion that party pacts are undemocratic, they may, in the future, become even more common as a means to address the iniquities of the first-past-the-post system. Indeed, in April 2022 Oliver Dowden, the Conservative Party Chairman, made suggestions that Labour and the Liberal Democrats had reached local party pacts to stand down candidates against each other in the May local elections.[2] Following the 2024 General Election, with the Conservatives and Reform splitting the right-wing vote to maximise the Labour landslide, the Conservatives again must face the prospect of coalition or 'fusion' to rebuild their electoral fortunes.

Notes

1 'Election Pacts: The Electoral Commission', https://www.electoralcommission.org.uk/election-pacts, accessed 1 May 2022.

2 Oliver Dowden to Sir Keir Starmer, 30 April 2022, https://twitter.com/OliverDowden/status/1520515882199486465, accessed 1 May 2022.

Select list of sources

Private papers and archives

Addison, Christopher, Bodleian Library
Ammon, Charles, Hull History Centre
Asquith, Herbert, Bodleian Library
Balfour, 1st Earl of, National Records of Scotland
Beaverbrook, 1st Baron, Parliamentary Archives
Birmingham Parliamentary Elections 1918–22, Local Studies and History Department, Birmingham Central Library
Bonar Law, Andrew, Parliamentary Archives
Bonham Carter, Lady Violet, Bodleian Library
Bridgeman, William, Shropshire Archives
British Pathé Film Archive
Bull, William, Churchill College Cambridge
Chamberlain, Austen, Cadbury Research Library: Special Collections, Birmingham University
Chamberlain, Neville, Cadbury Research Library: Special Collections, Birmingham University
Churchill, Winston, Churchill College Cambridge
Chatfield-Clarke, Sir Edgar, Isle of Wight Record Office.
Communist Party Archive, People's History Museum
Conservative Party Archive, Bodleian Library
Conservative and Unionist Association (Cambourne Division), Kresen Kernow
Conservative and Unionist Association (Lincoln Division), Lincolnshire Record Office
Conservative and Unionist Association (Ludlow Division), Shropshire Archives
Coombe Tennant, Winifred (South Glamorgan Archives Service)
Lloyd George, David, Parliamentary Archives
Lothian, 11th Marquess, National Records of Scotland
Gilmour, John, of Lundin, Fife and Montrave, South Walton, Renfrewshire National Records of Scotland
Hylton, 3rd Baron, Somerset Heritage Centre

Labour Party Archive, People's History Museum
Liberal Association (East Dorset), Dorset History Centre
National Archives
Newdegate, Francis, National Library of Australia
Palme Dutt, Rajani, People's History Museum
Ruggles-Brise, Edward, Essex Record Office
Scott, Leslie, Modern Records Centre, University of Warwick
Scovell, G. J. S., Lloyd George Archive
Templewood, 1st Viscount, Cambridge University Library
Underground Electric Railway Company Ltd, London Transport Museum
Weigall Manuscripts, Kent Archive Service
Wilson, Leslie, Fryer Library, University of Queensland
Weymss, Maynard Colchester, Gloucester Archives
Worthington-Evans, Laming, Bodleian Library

Contemporary publications, printed private papers, diaries, memoirs

Boyce, George, ed. *The Crisis of British Unionism: Lord Selborne's Domestic Political Papers, 1885–1922*. London: The Historians Press, 1987.

Clynes, J. R. *Memoirs 1869–1924*. London: Hutchinson & Co., 1937.

Gilbert, Martin, ed. *Winston S. Churchill: Companion Volume 4*, part 3. London: Heinemann, London, 1977.

Hoare, Samuel. *Empire of the Air*. London: Collins, 1967.

Humphreys, John H. *Practical Aspects of Electoral Reform: A Study of the General Election, 1922*. London: P. S. King & Son, 1923.

Middlemas, Keith, ed. *Thomas Jones: Whitehall Diary*, vols 1–3. London: Oxford University Press, 1969–71.

Ramsden, John, ed. *Real Old Tory Politics: The Political Diaries of Robert Sanders, Lord Bayford 1910–1935*. London: The Historians Press, 1984.

Riddell, Lord. *Lord Riddell's Intimate Diary of the Peace Conference and After 1918–1923*. London: Victor Gollancz, 1933.

Self, Robert, ed. *The Austen Chamberlain Diary Letters (1916–1937)*. Cambridge: Cambridge University Press, 1995.

Taylor, A. J. P., ed. *Lloyd George: A Diary by Frances Stevenson*. London: Hutchinson, 1971.

Thorpe, Andrew, and Richard Toye, eds. *Parliament and Politics in the Age of Asquith and Lloyd George: The Diaries of Cecil Harmsworth MP, 1909–1922*. Cambridge: Cambridge University Press, 2016.

Wilson, Trevor, ed. *The Political Diaries of C.P. Scott 1911–1928*. London: Collins, 1970.

Newspapers

Arbroath Herald
Belfast News-Letter
Belfast Telegraph
Chelmsford Chronicle
Cornubian and Redruth Times
Daily Express
Daily Mail
Daily Mirror
Dublin Evening Telegraph
Exeter and Plymouth Gazette
Daily Herald
Derby Daily Telegraph
Gloucestershire Echo
Gloucester Journal
Hampshire Independent
Hampshire Telegraph
Hull Daily Mail
Isle of Wight Observer
Leamington Spa Courier
Nottingham Journal
Pall Mall Gazette
Portsmouth Evening News
Reading Observer
The Scotsman
Sheffield Daily Telegraph
Sheffield Independent
South Notts Echo
Sunday Post
The Times
Western Daily Press
Western Mail

Western Morning News
The Western Morning News and Mercury
Westminster Gazette
Yorkshire Evening Post
Yorkshire Post and Leeds Intelligencer

Books

Adams, R. J. Q. *Bonar Law*. Stanford: Stanford University Press, 1999.

Adelman, Paul. *The Decline of the Liberal Party, 1910–1931*. London: Routledge, 1995.

Ball, Alan R. *British Political Parties: The Emergence of a Modern Party System*. London: Palgrave, 1987.

Ball, Stuart. *The Conservative Party and British Politics 1902–1951*. New York: Routledge, 2013.

Beaverbrook, Lord. *The Decline and Fall of Lloyd George*. New York: Duell, Sloan and Pearce, 1963.

Bentley, Michael. *The Liberal Mind, 1914–1929*. Cambridge: Cambridge University Press, 1977.

Blake, Robert. *The Conservative Party from Peel to Churchill*. London: Fontana, 1972.

Blake, Robert. *The Unknown Prime Minister: The Life and Times of Andrew Bonar Law 1858–1923*. London: Eyre and Spottiswoode, 1955.

Cook, Chris. *The Age of Alignment: Electoral Politics in Britain 1922–1929*. London: Macmillan, 1975.

Cook, Chris. *A Short History of the Liberal Party 1900–1984*. Basingstoke: Macmillan, 1984.

Cook, Chris, and John Stevenson. *A History of British Elections Since 1689*. London: Routledge, 2014.

Cowling, Maurice. *The Impact of Labour, 1920–1924: The Beginning of Modern British Politics*. Cambridge: Cambridge University Press, 1971.

Cregier, Don M. 'Lloyd George's Lucre: The National Liberal Fund'. In *Chiefs without Indians: Asquith, Lloyd George and the Liberal Remnant*, by Don M. Cregier, 113–47. Washington D.C.: University Press of America, 1982.

Cuthbert, D. D. 'Lloyd George and the Conservative Central Office, 1918–22'. In *Lloyd George: Twelve Essays*, edited by A. J. P. Taylor, 167–87. London: Hamilton, 1971.

Davies, S. *Liverpool Labour: Social and Political Influences on the Development of the Labour Party, 1900–1939*. Keele: Keele University Press, 1996.

Dutton, David. *A History of the Liberal Party Since 1900*, 2nd edition. Basingstoke: Palgrave, 2013.

Gilbert, Martin. *Winston S. Churchill. Official Biography, vol. 4: 1917–1922*. London: Heinemann, 1975.

Griffiths, Clare, *Labour and the Countryside: The Politics of Rural Britain, 1918–39* Oxford: Oxford University Press, 2007.

Holford, John. *Reshaping Labour: Organization, Work and Politics in Edinburgh in the Great War and After*. New York: Croom Helm, 1988.

Howell, David. *MacDonald's Party: Labour Identities and Crisis 1922–1931*. Oxford: Oxford University Press, 2002.

Jenkins, Roy. *The Chancellors*. London: Papermac, 1999.

Kinnear, Michael. *The Fall of Lloyd George: The Political Crisis of 1922*. London: Macmillan, 1973.

Koss, Stephen. *Asquith*. London: Allen Lane, 1976.

Laybourn, Keith, and Jack Reynold. *Liberalism and the Rise of Labour 1890–1918*. London: Croom Helm, 1984.

Leventhal, F. M. *Arthur Henderson*. Manchester: Manchester University Press, 1989.

Marquand, David. *Ramsay MacDonald*. London, Jonathan Cape, 1977.

McCrillis, Neal R. *The British Conservative Party in the Age of Universal Suffrage: Popular Conservatism, 1918–1929*. Columbus: Ohio State University Press, 1998.

McHugh, Declan. *Labour in the City: The Development of the Labour Party in Manchester, 1918–31*. Manchester: Manchester University Press, 2006.

McKibbin, Ross. *The Evolution of the Labour Party 1910–1924*. Oxford: Oxford University Press, 1974.

McLean, Ian. *The Legend of Red Clydeside*. Edinburgh: John Donald, 1983.

Morgan, Kenneth O. *Consensus and Disunity: The Lloyd George Coalition Government 1918–22*. Oxford: Clarendon Press, 1979.

Morgan, Kenneth O. 'Lloyd George's Stage Army: The Coalition Liberals, 1918–22'. In *Lloyd George: Twelve Essays*, edited by A. J. P. Taylor, 225–54. London: Hamilton, 1971.

Mowat, Charles Loch. *Britain Between the Wars*. London: Methuen, 1955.

Owen, Frank. *Tempestuous Journey: Lloyd George, His Life and Times*. London: Hutchinson, 1954.

Powell, David. *British Politics, 1910–35: The Crisis of the Party System*. London: Routledge, 2004.

Pugh, Martin. *Lloyd George*. London: Longman, 1988.

Pugh, Martin. *Speak for Britain! A New History of the Labour Party*. London: The Bodley Head, 2010.

Ramsden, John. *The Age of Balfour and Baldwin, 1902–1940*. London: Longman, 1978.

Ramsden, John. *An Appetite for Power: A History of the Conservative Party since 1830*. London: Harper Collins, 1998.

Rees, Rosemary. *Britain, 1890–1939*. London: Heinemann, 2003.

Searle, G. R. *A New England? Peace and War 1886–1918*. Oxford: Oxford University Press, 2004.

Tanner, Duncan. 'Class Voting and Radical Politics: The Liberal and Labour Parties, 1910–31'. In *Party, State and Society: Electoral Behaviour in Britain since 1920*, edited by Jon Lawrence and Miles Taylor, 106–30. Aldershot: Scolar, 1997.

Thackeray, David. *Conservatism for the Democratic Age: Conservative Cultures and the Challenge of Mass Politics in Early Twentieth Century England*. Manchester: Manchester University Press, 2013.

Thorpe, Andrew. *A History of the British Labour Party*. Basingstoke: Palgrave, 1997.

Tregidga, Gary. *The Liberal Party in South-West Britain Since 1918: Political Decline, Dormancy and Rebirth*. Exeter: University of Exeter Press, 2000.

Watts, Duncan. *Stanley Baldwin and the Search for Consensus*. London: Hodder and Stoughton, 1996.

Williams, Francis. *Fifty Years' March: The Rise of the Labour Party*. London: Odhams, 1950.

Wilson, Trevor. *The Downfall of the Liberal Party*. London: Collins, 1966.

Worley, Matthew. *The Foundations of the British Labour Party: Identities, Cultures and Perspectives 1900–39*. London: Routledge, 2016.

Worley, Matthew. *Labour's Grass Roots: Essays on the Activities of Local Labour Parties and Members, 1918–45*. London: Ashgate, 2005.

Wrigley, Chris. 'Coalition Blues: The Conservatives, the Liberals and Conservative-Liberal Coalitions in Britain since 1895'. In *The*

Foundations of the British Conservative Party: Essays on Conservatism from Lord Salisbury to David Cameron, edited by Bradley W. Hart and Richard Carr, 153–74. London: Bloomsbury, 2013.
Wrigley, Chris. *Lloyd George and the Challenge of Labour: The Post-War Coalition 1918–1922*. Hemel Hempstead: Harvester Wheatsheaf, 1990.

Articles

Beers, Laura D. 'Punting on the Thames: Electoral Betting in Interwar Britain', *Journal of Contemporary History* 45, no. 2 (2010): 282–314.
Close, David. 'Conservatives and Coalition after the First World War', *Journal of Modern History* 45, no. 2 (1973): 240–60.
Douglas, Roy. 'The Background to the "Coupon" Election Arrangements', *English Historical Review*, 86 (1971): 318–36.
Freeman, Gavin J. 'The Decline of the Liberal Party in the Heart of England: The Liberals in Leicestershire, 1914–24', *Historical Research* 89, no. 3 (2016): 531–49.
Freeman, Gavin J. 'The Liberal Party and the Impact of the 1918 Reform Act', *Parliamentary History* 37, no. 1 (2018): 47–63.
Graham Jones, J. 'The "Coaly Libs" and the "Wee Frees": Cardiganshire politics 1920–24', *Ceredigion*, Part 1 in 17, no. 3 (2015): 129–70, and Part 2 in 17, no. 4 (2016): 83–112.
McEwen, John M. 'The Coupon Election of 1918 and Unionist Members of Parliament', *Journal of Modern History* 34, no. 3 (1962): 294–306.
McGill, Barry. 'Lloyd George's Timing of the 1918 Election', *Journal of British Studies* 14, no. 1 (1974): 109–24.
Murray, Bruce. 'A New Age of Lloyd George Studies', *South African Historical Journal* 5, no. 1 (1973): 109–20.
Price, Emyr. 'Labour's "Breakthrough" in Caernarfon County in 1922: The Election of R T Jones to Westminster', *Caernarvonshire Historical Transactions* 64 (2003): 94–119.
Sloan, Geoffrey. 'Hide Seek and Negotiate: Alfred Cope and Counter Intelligence in Ireland 1919–1921', *Intelligence and National Security* 33, no. 2 (2018): 176–95.
Stanley, Luke. 'The Rebel Chief Whip: The Role of Leslie Wilson in the Fall of the Lloyd George Coalition, 1922', *Parliamentary History* 38, no. 2 (2019): 224–43.

Walker, William M. 'Dundee's Disenchantment with Churchill: A Comment upon the Downfall of the Liberal Party', *The Scottish Historical Review* 49, no. 147, Pt. 1 (1970): 85–108.

Wilson, Trevor. 'The Coupon and the British General Election of 1918', *Journal of Modern History* 36, no. 2 (1964): 28–42.

Unpublished theses

Kinnear, Michael. 'The British General Election of 1922', D.Phil, University of Oxford, 1965.

Index

www.ingramcontent.com/pod-product-compliance
Lightning Source LLC
LaVergne TN
LVHW052029300826
846742LV00025B/100